Skeletal remains from
The Cemetery of
St Nicholas Shambles
City of London

SKELETAL REMAINS FROM THE CEMETERY OF ST NICHOLAS SHAMBLES, CITY OF LONDON

William J. White

with contributions by Tony Dyson, Rosemary Powers, Sue Rivière, John Schofield, and the late Calvin Wells

Published by the London & Middlesex
Archaeological Society

First published 1988

Typeset and printed by BAS Printers Limited,
Over Wallop, Hampshire

Design and production: Melissa Denny of
Diptych

Cover artwork: Richard Lea

ISBN 0 903290 33 2

**The Society is grateful to English
Heritage for a grant towards the
publication of this Special Paper**

CONTENTS

ABSTRACT

234 articulated skeletons from the early medieval parish cemetery of St Nicholas Shambles, off Newgate Street in the City of London, were excavated by the Museum of London in 1975–7. They are dated archaeologically to the 11th and 12th centuries. Six grave-types were identified, though the majority were in simple graves. The presence of coffins could not be established with certainty, though fragments of wood were present in many graves.

Demographic and osteological data were compared with other medieval populations. Ranges and means of stature were consistent with comparable groups. The skulls provide a cranial form intermediate between Anglo-Saxon dolicephaly ('long-headed') and the later medieval bracycephaly ('round-headed'). Certain cranial and dental characteristics may suggest family subgroups in the population.

Evidence of disease on the bones was infrequent. Reconstruction of the dentition permitted an assessment to be made of the general health of the population. Nutritional disease in the form of osteoporosis did occur, bone defects being caused by anaemia possibly resulting from an iron-deficient diet. Osteoarthritis was found in many skeletons as a degenerative disease affecting most of the joints, but especially the vertebral column. One form of spinal degenerative disorder was four times more common in men than in women and may have been related to lifting activities. Cancerous tumours were few and not malignant. No evidence of infections such as tuberculosis was observed. Paget's disease was absent. In general few injuries suffered during life were apparent and fractures were relatively uncommon. Individual cases of note included a middle-aged man with a badly affected right arm, with a shoulder joint damaged through illness contracted probably during childhood. A younger man exhibited a developmental disorder that had interfered with the normal growth of his limbs. A girl with her left leg missing had survived to be a teenager and another, tall and probably overweight, had been left with a pronounced limp. Of particular note was the partial skeleton of a woman who died in childbirth. The high incidence of certain traits suggested that many of the skeletons were of related individuals. Analysis of the cemetery produced evidence for possible family groupings.

In advance of detailed publication of the excavation of the church and the topographical setting of the cemetery, a provisional discussion is offered of the various grave-types and possible evidence of grave-side ritual.

1. THE CEMETERY OF ST NICHOLAS SHAMBLES

John Schofield

with post-excavation analysis by Alan Thompson, Merry Hill and Sue Rivière

(a) Circumstances of excavation

(Figs 1, 2)

The land now occupied by the British Telecom Centre, Newgate Street (Figs 1, 2), was the site of several archaeological excavations by the Department of Urban Archaeology of the Museum of London in 1975–9. One of the major parts of the investigation concerned the small parish church of St Nicholas Shambles and its cemetery, largely to the north side of the church, in the south-west corner of the site adjacent to Newgate and King Edward Streets.[1] This area was first examined after demolition of those parts of the 19th-century GPO Headquarters Building (hence the site-code GPO75) which had survived damage in World War II. At first only a limited area was made available, but by 1979 the greater part of the church had been exposed, leaving only the west end beneath King Edward Street (which had been widened several times since the medieval period) and the south side close to and beneath the northern pavement of Newgate Street. To the north of the church an area approximately 21 m × 17 m comprising the northern cemetery was excavated; skeletons were also uncovered to the east of the church. Although the area of excavation was dictated by modern boundaries, it seems clear from documentary evidence (below, p.8) that the excavation comprised nearly all the cemetery area on the north and east sides of the church.

The study of the cemetery properly forms part of a comprehensive study of the medieval church and its surroundings which is in preparation,[2] but which, it was felt, should not hold up publication of the skeletal information. The Museum has therefore decided to preface Mr White's report with a provisional summary of relevant matters: documentary evidence, an outline of the archaeological phasing of the church, the nature of the

2. Location of the site in Newgate Street, showing the area of excavation of the church and cemetery (GPO 75).

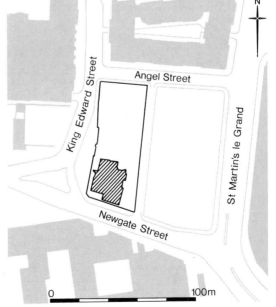

1. Location of the site in the modern City of London.

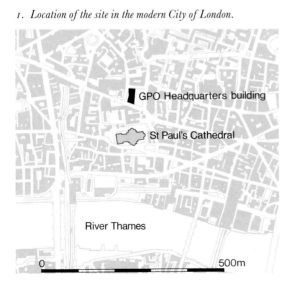

excavation of the graveyard, and a brief description and discussion of the more unusual grave-types and burial customs found in the cemetery in order to refine, if possible, the stratigraphic date of the burials. All these aspects will be dealt with in greater detail in the final report on the church and the graveyard, when post-excavation analysis on a wider scale has been carried out.

(b) Documentary evidence for the church of St Nicholas and the cemetery

Tony Dyson

(Fig 2)

The church of St Nicholas Shambles is first recorded in 1187, and possibly *c*.1144. From documentary evidence of the 16th century and later, the church and churchyard appear to have occupied an area roughly 30 m square, bounded by Chicken or Butcher's Hall Lane (King Edward Street) to the west and Newgate Street to the south. The eastern boundary was formed by the backs of houses which fronted onto Pentecost or Pincocke Lane (later Bath, or Roman Bath, Street). From the outset of the 14th century the churchyard was bounded to the north by the garden of the Greyfriars, which extended across Chicken Lane, enclosed north of this point, to Pentecost Lane and beyond. There is no evidence that the western or southern limits of the site were ever used for burials; shops and stalls are recorded here from the 14th century. It is possible that, before the church was extended in the 13th and later centuries, the churchyard east of the church was used for burials, but the evidence of the early 16th century, coinciding with the abandonment of the church, strongly suggests that the cemetery was confined to an area between the church itself and the boundary with the Greyfriar's garden to the north, amounting to a maximum of 162.6 sq m.

Documentary references to the church and to burials within it, which include mention of chapels, date from the 14th century at the earliest; since the archaeological date of the burials excavated in the cemetery is placed in the 11th/12th centuries, these references will be reserved for the final report concerning the church. Similarly the closure of the church in 1548–51 and the rebuilding of its site into Bull Head Court will be deferred to a later publication.

(c) Archaeological evidence for the church of St Nicholas

Sue Rivière

(Fig 5)

The excavated fragments of the church of St Nicholas comprised foundations only; no walls or floor levels survived. Six periods of construction were apparent:

Phase 1: the earliest church comprised a nave and slightly thinner chancel.
Phase 2: the chancel was extended in a narrower form.
Phase 3: a north aisle was added to the nave and former chancel areas.
Phase 4: the north aisle was extended to the east end.
Phase 5: the east end was rebuilt, possibly at the same time as the rebuilding of the eastern part of the north aisle.
Phase 6: various foundations were added to the north and south of the church, including a possible vestry near the north-east corner of the church.

Considered dates for these phases await detailed reconsideration of the stratigraphic and dating evidence, but provisionally Phase 1 is placed in the 11th century, Phase 2 in the second half of the 12th century or later, Phase 3 in the late 13th century and Phases 4–6 in the period late 13th century–1548.

The outlines of the first, second and final (sixth) periods of construction are shown in Figs 5–11. The question of how best to reconstruct the southern side of the church, from the meagre archaeological and documentary evidence, will be addressed in the separate report on the church.

(d) Survival of strata and date of the cemetery

(Figs 3–4)

The methods of recording and excavation on site have been described in detail elsewhere.[3] Skeletons were not planned *in situ* but were photographed from above the pelvic area, and two tags at the extremities of the surviving bones (often the head and feet) were planned as co-ordinates on the site grid. Plans were drawn, when required, at a later stage from the photographs. Skeletons were lifted and bagged individually, with skulls generally in separate boxes. Scatters of disarticulated bone were not photographed or planned, but recorded with pottery and other finds from the relevant contexts.

Though the cemetery was excavated by open-area methods it was rarely possibly to establish grave-cuts and therefore stratigraphic relationships between burials; a difficulty experienced elsewhere in the excavation of cemeteries.[4] Because medieval ground levels were completely absent due to the depth of 19th century basements, it was also difficult to relate burials to the fabric of the church except where certain foundations cut or were cut by burials. None of the graves produced closely datable contemporary objects; a number of Roman coins in the cemetery soil were residual. Ceramic dates of the 11th to 12th century (with little pottery post-dating about 1180) were obtained from the cemetery soils.[5] Beneath the burials, a number of pits had been dug immediately north of the north side of the

earliest church, presumably reflecting secular activity on the graveyard's border with Stinking Lane (King Edward Street); these pits produced 10th–12th century pottery. The intrinsic date of the excavated portion of the cemetery is therefore of the 11th–12th centuries.

Because of the absence of stratigraphic links, the burials which were recorded within the north aisle could be either early external burials later incorporated within the body of the church by the building of the aisle, or burials made within the aisle after its construction. It is suggested that the burials are likely to be early and to precede the construction of the aisle (placed in Phase 3 of the church's life, see above, p.8), using two arguments: (a) that the general depth of the surviving strata in relation to inferred medieval ground level suggests that the surviving strata comprised the lower, older part of the cemetery, and (b) the positions of the burials suggest a direct relationship with the first two phases of the church, provisionally of 11th–12th century date, therefore preceding the construction of the north aisle.

Firstly, it is clear that only the lowest portion of the cemetery survived to be recorded. The adjacent church had been reduced to its foundations

3. General view to the north during excavation, showing the nature of the intrusions by foundations for Bull Head Court and the 19th century GPO Headquarters building.

by later building, first by that of the houses of Bull Head Court immediately after the demolition of the church in 1548–51, and more especially by the construction of the GPO Building in 1870. The projected curvature of arches in some of the foundation fragments suggests that early medieval ground level was 0.8–1.0 m above the top of the surviving strata which reached about 14.00 m OD. A late 13th century ground level of 16.00 m OD was recorded within the Greyfriars' church, about 30 m to the west, in 1973.[6] A late 17th century ground level a further 1 m higher can be inferred from the Wren rebuilding of Christ Church Greyfriars, although raising of the ground after the Great Fire may have intervened. It is therefore likely that the excavated portion comprised only the bottom 1 m of a cemetery which was some 4 m thick by the time of its closure in 1548–51. Given the shallowness of early medieval burials in general,[7] this would strengthen a suggestion that the burials excavated here tend to belong to the early history of the church and cemetery, in the 11th and 12th centuries, though later intrusion cannot be discounted.

Secondly, the distribution of the recorded burials avoids the areas of the Phase 1 nave and chancel (Fig 5). Although these internal areas were damaged by later intrusion, enough pre-church strata survived to suggest that burials were never dug within the nave and chancel to the absolute depth of the burials surviving outside them. But it seems unlikely that these areas would have survived to 1548–51 without any burials in them. A conclusion must be that later burials did not reach this depth, and were removed in later centuries. This in turn reinforces the suggestion that the recorded burials are of one general and early date, lying outside the first church. Plans showing the extent of the burials are given here in Figs 5–11; Figs 6–7 show distribution by sex, Figs 8–11 by age.

Slumping into the underlying Roman strata was particularly noticeable in the eastern half of the cemetery. This has given an apparent density of burials to this area. This misleading density renders conclusions from distribution maps of skeletons with particular characteristics somewhat difficult. Definite rows of burials and there-

4. General conditions of survival, showing skeletons 5047, 5048 and 5058.

King Edward Street

Final church

First church

Second church

?South aisle

Site boundary in 1975

Outline of property surveyed in 1862

Newgate Street

N

0   10m

*5. Plan showing distribution of all recorded burials. The length
of the symbol indicates the extent of the surviving remains. The
tone in this and Figs 6–11 and 34 indicates excavated areas.*

6. *Plan showing distribution of male burials. The length of* *refer to skeletons of individual note mentioned in the text.*
the symbol indicates the extent of the surviving remains. Numbers

7. *Plan showing distribution of female burials. The length of the symbol indicates the extent of the surviving remains. Numbers refer to skeletons of individual note mentioned in the text.*

8. Plan showing distribution of burials of juveniles (3–12 years old and infants of 2 years old or less). The length of the symbol indicates the extent of the surviving remains. Numbers refer to skeletons of individual note mentioned in the text.

N

5169

5193

5152

5120

Final church
5081

First church

Second church

King Edward Street

Site boundary in 1975

?South aisle

Outline of property surveyed in 1862

Newgate Street

0   10m

9. *Plan showing distribution of burials of adolescents (13–16 years old). The length of the symbol indicates the extent of the surviving remains. Numbers refer to skeletons of individual note mentioned in the text.*

10. *Plan showing distribution of burials of young adults (17–25 years old). The length of the symbol indicates the extent of the surviving remains. Numbers refer to skeletons of individual note mentioned in the text.*

11. *Plan showing distribution of burials of mature adults (over 26 years old). The length of the symbol indicates the extent of the surviving remains. Numbers refer to skeletons of individual note mentioned in the text.*

fore perhaps pathways through the cemetery were not readily apparent; this question will be re-examined when the sites of probable doors into the church have been identified in the church report.

(e) Burial types and burial practices

(Figs 12–29)

A total of 234 skeletons form the basis of the following analyses. The majority of these were fairly intact, but disturbances and subsequent burial had removed parts of others (for the general conditions of survival, see Figs 3–4); thus the grouping by burial type cannot hope to be totally precise. A distinction has been made here between burial type or practice (concerned with the nature of the grave and coffin) and possible evidence of burial ritual (the addition of certain materials to the burial, particularly loose stones and pebbles in the mouth). The position of the hands within the burials does not seem to vary significantly.

(I) BURIAL TYPES:

A basic and most numerous type of burial (I) and five specialised variants (II to VI) were recorded. These were:

Type I (189 cases; Figs 13–16) a simple burial, perhaps in a coffin. Due to difficulties of definition in excavation, it was not usually possible to determine whether these burials were in coffins or not, though in some few cases it seemed likely from gravecuts when observed. Nails were occasionally found near a skeleton; in certain other cases traces of wood may have represented coffins, or head-markers, or merely pieces of wood used in the burial. A further sub-group of graves had floors of pebbles. One adult female burial of this type (5050) retained fragments of cloth, possibly flax, adhering to the skull; apparently the traces of a linen shroud.[8]

Type II (22 cases; Figs 18–21): graves with stone pillows. The skeletons in these graves represented three old men (5165, 5215, 5229), two neonates (5210, 5227), two adult men (5042, 5172) and 15 adult women (5053, 5072, 5094, 5116, 5133, 5148, 5150, 5168, 5186, 5190, 5193, 5194, 5203, 5233, 5311).

Type III (10 cases; Fig 22): graves with a floor of crushed chalk and mortar. Three skeletons of this burial type were adult male (5070, 5118, 5304); the other seven female, six adult and one juvenile (5073, 5144, 5147, 5257, 5294, 5307; 5310).

Type IV (eight cases; Figs 23–4): cists formed of mortared stones, or simply lined with chalk and mortar. Of the skeletons in these graves, two (5176, 5306) were male, two (5125, 5134) female, and four (5103, 5126, 5290, 5305) indeterminate; there were six adults, one juvenile and one child of 2–3 years.

Type V (one case; Fig 26): charcoal burial. The body (5322, an infant of indeterminate sex) was

12. *Summary of burial types I–VI.*

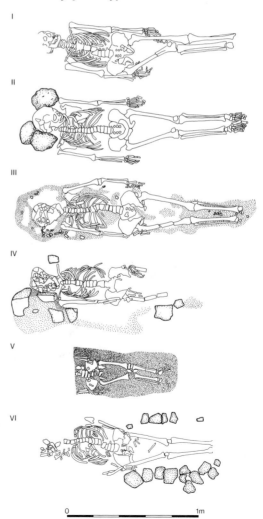

I

II

III

IV

V

VI

0   1m

laid on a bed of charcoal and more charcoal was placed on the body, completely enclosing it.

Type VI (four cases; Fig 27): graves lined with dry-laid stone or tile. In two cases the skeletons were of adult women (5101, 5238), and in two cases adult men (5108, 5234). Some of the lining was distinctly casual or peremptory.

Type I (simple graves) and Type III (simple graves with chalk and mortar floors)

The lack of more detailed information inhibits extended discussion of the most numerous grave-type (I). Wooden coffins are known at Repton from 'probably the 7th century',[9] at Barton-on-Humber in the pre-9th century cemetery,[10] at

13. *Burial Type I, skeleton 5050.*

14. *Burial Type I, skeleton 5064.*

15. *Burial Type I, skeleton 5068.*

16. Burial Type I, skeleton 5109.

17. Burial Type I, skeleton 5112.

Hereford in the 9th/early 10th century,[11] and have been presumed from the attitude of the burials at Raunds (Northants) in the 10th and 11th centuries.[12] At St Nicholas, nails may have derived from the underlying Roman strata or even from activities within the Saxon-period dark earth layer into which the burials were cut.[13] The fortuitous survival of a fragment of what was probably a shroud in one female grave (skeleton 5050) suggests that other examples may have been present. Linen shrouds were a common feature of female burial in the medieval period, whereas men were sometimes buried in hairshirts woven from coarse two-ply yarn.[14]

Type III burials, involving a chalk and mortar floor, may be a variant of the simple burial; graves with chalk floors are found occasionally in both Roman and medieval cemeteries. One grave with a floor of limestone rubble was recorded at

the ?11th century cemetery of St Mark's, Lincoln;[15] at the 11th-century church beneath the bailey of Norwich Castle graves may have been capped with chalk,[16] perhaps an analogous practice.

Type II (pillow graves)

The pillow-graves of Type II were occupied by adult women in two-thirds of the examples. This contrasts with the findings at Raunds, where in the 10th century cemetery one third of the 339 *in situ* burials had pillows, and the majority contained men.[17] Although at Barton-on-Humber stones were placed on either side of the head within a wooden coffin in at least one case,[18] the St Nicholas examples appear to suggest burial without a coffin. At St Helen's, York, several graves 'presumably for uncoffined burials' outside

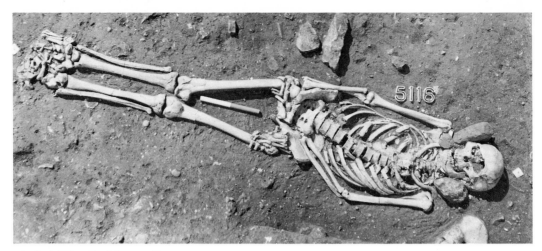

18. Burial Type II, skeleton 5116.

19. Burial Type II, skeleton 5133.

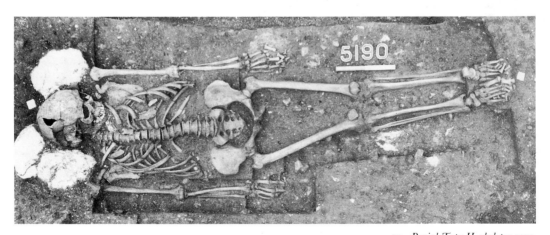

20. Burial Type II, skeleton 5190.

the church had limestone blocks along the western ends to protect the skull.[19] At Hereford pillows were used in three charcoal burials, and one ordinary burial, in a later phase of the cemetery, dating to the latter half of the 10th or the 11th century;[20] at St Alban's all graves found beneath the chapter-house in the pre-1088 late Saxon cemetery were pillow-graves, all in this

21. *Burial Type II, skeleton 5227*

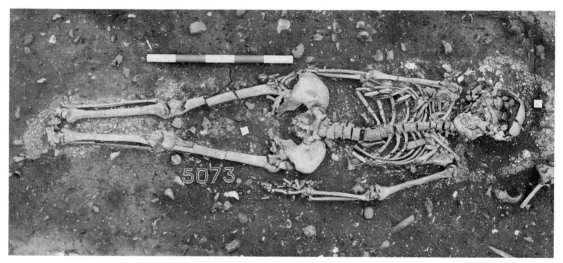

22. *Burial Type III, skeleton 5073.*

case male.[21] At St Oswald's Priory, Gloucester, pillow-graves seemed to be of 10th/11th century date;[22] the 11th-century cemetery beneath the castle bailey at Norwich contained several pillow-graves, especially in children's burials.[23] The practice would seem to have faded out during or after the 13th century. At Winchester a few pillow-graves were found in the Saxon cemetery associated with the Cathedral, occurring sporadically from the early 9th to the early/mid 11th centuries; but none were found in the 900 graves of the medieval cemetery.[24] At St Mary's Church, Stow (Lincs), however, at least one 13th century grave contained a stone pillow.[25]

Type IV (stone and mortar cists) and Type VI (dry-laid stone)

The stone and mortar cists (IV) displayed a range of proportions ranging between many stones lightly mortared and a grave lined entirely with mortar. Such a variety is found also on the other London sites where such cists have been recorded. Using dry-laid stone (VI) to line a grave, or possibly to pack it after the insertion of the coffin, may be a variant of the same practice. Laying stones or tiles around the body is known at several late and sub-Roman cemeteries: it seems to become common on late 4th century sites, as at Lankhills, Winchester.[26] At St Alban's some of the coffins of the mid-4th century Roman cemetery were packed on the outside with flints. The custom continued in early Christian times: a cist of 'concrete' and pounded brick, roofed with what were probably imbrices, and containing a wooden coffin was found beneath a wall in the churchyard of St Dunstan in the East in London in 1824, and was compared by Wheeler to the

23. Burial Type IV, skeleton 5103.

24. Burial Type IV, skeleton 5125.

25. Burial Type IV, skeleton 5176.

burials of the early archbishops at St Augustine's, Canterbury.[27] Stone-lined cists have been found on a number of continental church sites, e.g. near St Peter's, Zurich, dated to the mid 7th to end of 8th century.[28] A chalk-lined grave containing a skeleton found on the north side of St Paul's Cathedral in 1841–3 may have been associated with a trial die or weight datable to the mid 9th-century.[29]

Stone-lined graves of Types IV/VI were perhaps a less prestigious imitation of stone sarcophagi or one-piece stone coffins, and as such comprised an equally long tradition. Monolithic coffins were used in burials at Old Minster, Winchester, in the 10th/11th centuries.[30] In London, Roman sarcophagi were re-used; possibly for the burial of Sebbi, the first Christian King of Essex, at St Paul's in 694[31] and for a Saxon or early

26. *Burial Type V, skeleton 5322.*

27. *Burial Type VI, skeleton 5101.*

medieval burial at Westminster Abbey.[32]

The dating of the stone- or mortar-lined grave is vague at present due to the broad date ranges of some of the examples; the form is found alongside major churches of Saxon or Norman foundation, but the end of the period of use is unclear. Several cases are known from monastic sites of the late 11th and 12th centuries: Bermondsey Abbey (where two examples were cut by the foundations of the 12th century church);[33] Holy Trinity Priory Aldgate[34] and St John's Colchester[35] (here possibly later than 12th century also). They are also known from late Saxon or Saxo-Norman parish church sites in London: St Bride's Fleet Street[36] (pre-12th century) and the graveyard (? of the pre-priory church) beneath the south side of the 12th-century priory church at Holy Trinity Priory, Aldgate,[37] (late Saxon, possibly 11th century). At St Guthlac's Minster in Hereford stone-lined cists were dated to the first half of the 12th century[38] though on this site the removal of the burial ground to the present cathedral in the middle of the century does not allow any suggestion about the time-span of the practice to be made. At the comparable 11th-century church beneath the bailey at Norwich two graves were lined with loose large flints, in one case clearly added after partial backfilling.[39]

The lined cist grave continued to be used in the medieval period in prestigious locations, such as near chapels or shrines. At the Lady Chapel-by-the-Cloister, Wells, cists and stone coffins were recorded.[40] At Winchester in the Anglo-Saxon Old Minster cemetery chalk and limestone lined cists first appeared in the 11th century. Mortared cists are rare in the medieval cemetery, and are only found in the earliest, 13th-century generation of graves. Unmortared chalk cists first appear in the same generation and continue throughout the medieval period, forming about half of the *c*. 900 graves found north of the Cathedral around St Swithun's tomb and chapel.[41]

A tentative conclusion may be that stone-lined cists, and possibly their humbler dry-laid variant, while apparently a recurring practice, were more common in the 11th and 12th centuries. They probably indicate some greater care and prestige in the burial; though at Winchester, 'the cist graves were by no means necessarily the more important group' since of twenty graves apparently of priests, furnished with chalice or chalice and patten, only nine were of cist type.[42] It should also be emphasised that at St Nicholas cists were the exception, in contrast, for instance, to the ?11th century cemetery on the south side of Holy Trinity Priory Aldgate, where in time cists became the dominant burial type.[43] It seems likely that cists were an exceptional and rare occurrence in small neighbourhood cemeteries; at St Mark's, Lincoln, for instance, only one cist, dating to a period earlier than the second quarter of the 12th century, was recorded among 202 burials in the early medieval phases.[44]

Type V (charcoal burial)

One charcoal burial (V) was recorded. It comprised the disturbed lower part of a young person. Charcoal burials are recorded in cemeteries of the Saxon period, probably of the 9th century at St Frideswide's, Oxford,[45] and Romsey Abbey;[46] in two periods, of 800–950 and 900–1100, at St Guthlac's Minster, Hereford;[47] in the 10th/11th century cemetery at Old Minster, Winchester;[48] in the cemetery of c.900–c.1086 at St Oswald's Priory, Gloucester;[49] in the 11th century at St Wystan's, Repton;[50] the 11th and 12th centuries at St Mark's, Lincoln;[51] and over 50 were recorded in the cemetery dating from the 9th century to the early 12th alongside the church near the west end of Exeter Cathedral.[52] At least one charcoal burial was found at the parish cemetery of St Helen's, York, dating probably from the 12th century;[53] but they must be counted a comparative rarity from early medieval parish church

cemeteries.[54] The significance of the practice remains unknown.

(II) EVIDENCE OF BURIAL RITUAL

There was evidence of two further occasional burial practices. In three cases stones or pieces of Roman tile were laid on the body—one in a plain grave (5292), one in a pillow-grave (5172) (Fig 28), and one in a stone-lined cist (5305). The single burial recorded with stones on either side of the head at St Bride's[55] also had a piece of Roman tile on the chest. Stones laid on parts of the body, including over the head and face, were recorded at Raunds; and an example of flints being added to the side of the grave during back-filling at Norwich in the 11th century has already been noted (p.24).

Secondly, in four further cases (skeletons 5189, 5192, 5195, 5240) a pebble had been placed in the mouth (Fig 29); all in simple Type I graves. The skeletons were of one mature man (aged 35–8) and three comparatively elderly women (aged 38–41, 45 +, and 42–5 respectively). The practice of placing a stone in the mouth occurs once at Raunds, in a male of 17–25 who had contracted poliomyelitis in his youth and subsequently suffered tuberculosis; the pathology of the St Nicholas examples is however unremarkable.

It seems likely that these two practices reflect some kind of religious belief or even graveside ritual, for which the stone pillows may also have been employed. In this regard it may be relevant

28. Stones laid on the body, skeleton 5172.

29. Pebble in the mouth, skeleton 5053.

that part of the funerary rites in early medieval times was carried out at the graveside. A payment called 'soul-scot' was paid 'to the minster to which it [the soul] belongs' in King Edgar's code of 959–63[56] and in the laws of Ethelred (1008) 'soul-scot should be paid at the open grave'.[57]

Conclusions: burial types and rituals

Forty-five of the 234 articulated burials, or 19%, showed special care in the preparation of the grave. These abnormal types (II–VI) can be paralleled elsewhere in larger and smaller late Saxon and early medieval churches; present knowledge, though fragmentary, suggests a general date-span in England of 9th–12th centuries for these customs. Further work on the St Nicholas and other sites may clarify the date-ranges of the individual burial types. Although the numbers at St Nicholas were small, the apparent reverence with which old women were often treated—the pillow-grave, and the pebble in the mouth—is notable.

Footnotes and references

1. The excavation was directed by Alan Thompson, under the general supervision of Field Officers David Browne and, later, Charles Hill. The excavation and recording of the skeletons was ably carried out by Hilary Kent, Merry Morgan Hill and others. The excavation was funded by the Department of the Environment, and took place by kind permission of the Post Office (later British Telecom).

2. J. Schofield (ed) *The Early Church in London*, in preparation. Preliminary post-excavation analysis by Sue Rivière has indicated that such questions as the relationship between burials and each phase of the church, including whether burials preceded the first stone church, may be fruitfully attempted. Burials have also been arranged, where possible, in strings of stratigraphic succession up to 14 burials deep, but the analysis is not fine enough to warrant sub-division of the cemetery group.

3. M. Morgan, 'Excavation and recording techniques used at the cemetery of St Nicholas Shambles, London' *London Archaeol* 3 (1978) 213–6.

4. B. Kjølbye-Biddle, 'A cathedral cemetery: problems in excavation and interpretation' *World Archaeol* 7 (1975) 89–91; J.D. Dawes & J.R. Magilton *The Cemetery of St Helen-on-the-Walls, Aldwark, York* The Archaeology of York 10/1 (1980), 3.

5. Dating of the pottery by Alan Vince.

6. T. Johnson, 'Excavations at Christchurch, Newgate, 1973' *Trans Lon Middx Archaeol Soc* 25 (1974) 225.

7. On cemetery sites in the City of London the surface from which graves are cut is normally not present, since the graves are often cut into by subsequent ones, or truncation has taken place during modern building works. Late Saxon graves cut from a ground-surface excavated at the Holy Trinity Priory site (LEA84) in 1984 were generally 0.4 m deep (S. Rivière, pers comm). Where burials at the late Saxon cemetery at Raunds could be related to the original ground-surface, the adult graves averaged 0.44 m in depth (A. Boddington, pers comm). Graves at the medieval cemetery at Winchester Cathedral were up to 1 m deep (Kjølbye-Biddle, *op. cit.* in note 4, Fig 20).

8. Frances Pritchard notes: the fragment is ?flax, single, Z-spun yarn; tabby weave, slightly open textured; 15–16/13–14 threads per 10 mm (registered accession GPO75 967).

9. M. Biddle, pers comm.

10. W. Rodwell, pers comm.

11. R. Shoesmith, *Excavations at Castle Green*, Hereford

City Excavations I, CBA Research Report 36 (1980), 27.

12. A. Boddington, pers comm.

13. From Winchester (Old Minster and New Minster cemeteries) coffin nails were found *in situ* from the early 8th to the late 11th century; but none *in situ* in the medieval cemetery (B. Kjølbye-Biddle, pers comm).

14. E. Crowfoot, 'The textiles', in T. G. Hassall (ed) 'Excavations at Oxford Castle, 1965–1973' *Oxoniensia* 41 (1976), 271–274, esp 273.

15. B.J.J. Gilmour & D.A. Stocker, *St Mark's Church and Cemetery* The Archaeology of Lincoln XIII-1 (1986), 16.

16. B. Ayers, *Excavations within the North-East Bailey of Norwich Castle, 1979*, E Anglian Archaeol 28 (1985), 19.

17. A. Boddington, pers comm.

18. W. Rodwell, *Archaeology of the English Church* (1981), Fig 71.

19. Dawes & Magilton, *op. cit.* in note 4, 15.

20. Shoesmith, *op. cit.* in note 11, 29.

21. B. Kjølbye-Biddle, pers comm.

22. C.M. Heighway, 'Excavations at Gloucester: 5th Interim Report, St Oswald's Priory 1977–8' *Antiq J* 40 (1980), 217.

23. Ayers, *op. cit.* in note 16, 19.

24. B. Kjølbye-Biddle, pers comm.

25. P. Fairweather, 'Excavation Report: St Mary's Church, Stow, Lincolnshire' *Bulletin of International Soc for the Study of Church Monuments* 10 (1984), 218.

26. G. Clarke, *Pre-Roman and Roman Winchester Part II: The Roman Cemetery at Lankhills* (1979), 355.

27. RCHM *London III: Roman* (1928), 139.

28. J. Hanser *et al*, *Das Neue Bild des alten Zurich* (Zurich, 1983), 44–6.

29. *Gents Mag* 1841 II, 264–5, 499. The coin-die (or weight) was however not found in clear association with the grave.

30. Kjølbye-Biddle, *op. cit.* in note 4, 105–6.

31. Bede, *Historia Ecclesiastica* VI, 11 as suggested by R. Merrifield, *London City of the Romans* (1983), 280, n61.

32. RCHM *London I: Westminster Abbey* (1924), 81.

33. W.F. Grimes, *The Excavation of Roman and Medieval London* (1968), pl 101.

34. J. Schofield, 'Excavations at Holy Trinity Priory, Aldgate, 1979', DUA Archive Report (1985).

35. P. Crummy, *Aspects of Anglo-Saxon and Norman Colchester* CBA Research Report 39 (1981), 45 and Fig 37.

36. Grimes, *op. cit.* in note 33, 185, pl 83.

37. S. Rivière, 'Excavations at Mitre Street' *Popular Archaeol* 6 No.14 (December 1985/January 1986) 37–41.

38. Shoesmith, *op. cit.* in note 11, 29.

39. Ayers, *op. cit.* in note 16, 19.

40. Rodwell, *op. cit.* in note 18, 153 and pl 72.

41. B. Kjølbye-Biddle, pers comm.

42. Kjølbye-Biddle, *op. cit.* in note 4, 91.

43. Rivière, *op. cit.* in note 37.

44. Gilmour & Stocker, *op. cit.* in note 15, 20.

45. J. Schofield and D. Palliser (eds) *Recent Archaeological Research in English Towns*, CBA (1981), 81.

46. *ibid*, 86.

47. Shoesmith, *op. cit.* in note 11, 29.

48. Kjølbye-Biddle, *op. cit.* in note 4, 105–7.

49. Heighway, *op. cit.* in note 22, 217.

50. B.Kjølbye-Biddle, pers comm.

51. Gilmour & Stocker, *op. cit.* in note 15, 16, 20.

52. Schofield & Palliser, *op. cit.* in note 45, 37; D. Henderson, pers comm.

53. Dawes & Magilton, *op. cit.* in note 4, 16.

54. B. Kjølbye-Biddle, pers comm.

55. Grimes, *op. cit.* in note 33, pl 81.

56. D. Whitelock (ed) *English Historical Documents I: c.500–1042* (2nd ed, 1979), 431–2.

57. B. Thorpe *Ancient Laws and Institutes of England* (1840), i, 309; D. Whitelock, M. Brett & C.N.L. Brooke (eds), *Councils and Synods* (1981), 369. For the general context of the payment in parish life of the 11th century, see F. Barlow, *The English Church 1000–1066* (2nd ed, 1979), 196–8.

2. THE HUMAN BONES: SKELETAL ANALYSIS

William J. White

(a) Laboratory procedure

The human bones were examined after having been lifted carefully and hardened by drying off on site at ambient temperature, with further cleaning where appropriate. The state of preservation was uneven but the general assessment made of the overall condition of the bones was 'fair'. In a minority of cases neither washing nor brushing had proved possible owing to the friable nature of the skeletal remains and these were presented in the original soil matrix (with or without consolidation with polyvinyl acetate). When of diagnostic importance broken bones were repaired (by being cemented together) with a suitable adhesive.[1]

The results of the examination were recorded on data sheets of standard form and complemented the information logged during excavation of the site.[2] Similarly, for each of the articulated skeletons excavated, the various bones present were plotted on the stylised skeletal diagram depicted on the standard burial-recording *pro forma*. Comparison of the latter with the photographic record of the same burial, made at the time of exposure, provided supplementary information about the disposition of the skeleton and of the displacement of certain bones from anatomical position by post-burial processes such as putrefactive decay or the action of burrowing animals.[3]

Assessment of gender and age at death was undertaken for the human skeletal remains using the currently accepted techniques.[4] Unfortunately, however, the fragmentary nature of certain of the burials excavated (and of the unstratified material, in particular) frequently meant that less than the full range of criteria for the determination of sex and age could be applied.

In the estimation of the sex of the deceased the chief diagnostic features of both skull and pelvis were often absent and, therefore, recourse to the evidence of sexual dimorphism as evident elsewhere in the skeleton became necessary.[5] Attempts were made to avoid subjective visual judgements based upon the relative robustness and muscularity of the skeleton in favour of measurements made upon certain bones in an effort to discriminate between the sexes by means of differential bone dimensions.[6] The sexing of sub-adults, in particular, remained problematical. Where a patent pre-auricular sulcus was evident on the ilium the remains were classed as female.[7] Otherwise, the dimensions of the diameter of the lower permanent canine tooth, when present in the juvenile jaw, assumed predominance in gender-diagnosis.[8] Nonetheless, in a number of instances, unequivocal assignment of gender proved elusive. Here, it was decided that the fragmentary skeletal material would be subjected to *citrate* analysis.[9] This work of sex-estimation is in progress and will be reported separately.

Age assessment based similarly on the characteristics of the skull and pelvis (*viz.* dental development and attrition, fusion of the cranial sutures, condition of development of the pubic symphysis, etc) suffered in equal measure when these regions of the skeleton were lacking. As usual, for the younger members of the population, there was supplementary information in the form both of the state of epiphyseal union and of the measured lengths of the diaphyses. The latter approach has been employed at a number of archaeological sites and, here, medieval England has been served well by the work of Miss Rosemary Powers of the British Museum (Natural History) (see Appendix 4).[10] Hence, comparison of the bone-shaft length measurements with the data collected and tabulated in other published series, and with child skeletons of the established age from the cemetery itself, permitted the ageing of the headless sub-adults. On the other hand, although those adults who had retained their teeth were ageable in accordance with the published general scheme for molar tooth attrition in British medieval skulls, the paucity of aged and sexed jaws in the diagnostic sub-groups precluded an internal attrition-rate classification for the site.[11] This failing served to underline the general risk of under-ageing inherent even in complete skeletons.[12] Indeed, for fragmentary adult skeletons, frequently the sole criterion for ageing available was epiphyseal fusion, merely rendering them as adults over the age of 25 years. Here, greater precision in age-determination awaited the microscopic analysis of the cortical characters of the long bones.[13] This research, too, is in progress and its results will be reported in due course.

Individual skeletal measurements were determined by standard techniques using conventional equipment. For immature persons diaphyseal lengths and iliac diameters were measured and, for adults, not only the maximum lengths of the long bones but also their relevant diameters. Unfortunately, most of the surviving skulls were damaged or distorted beyond hope of useful reconstruction and comparatively few were sufficiently well preserved for cranial measurements to be taken. Trotter and Gleser's formulae (devised 1952, revised 1958) were used to calculate the stature of adults.[14] In accordance with current anthropometric practice no attempt was made to estimate height for children, although long bone lengths with the epiphyses glued into place were substituted into the above formulae in order to arrive at the stature-estimation of adolescents, as practised at York.[15]

Genetic evidence was sought by surveying the raw material for discontinuous traits, chiefly in the skull, but also (where possible) in the post cranial remains. The former included patent metopic suture, wormian bones, tori, supra-orbital and parietal foramina in addition to congenital anomalies of the teeth. Other non-metric skeletal variables included a septal aperture (or trochlear foramen) at the distal end of the humerus, congenital fusion of the cervical vertebrae, separate neural arches of the fifth lumbar vertebrae, lumbo-sacralisation of lumbar vertebrae, spina bifida occulta and the presence, fusion or absence of other congenital traits.

Despite the frequent comminution of skulls, where any portion of the jaws was preserved (however fragmentarily), the dentition was mapped.[16] The standard *pro forma* was used also to record the dental data: presence or absence of teeth, condition of roots and crowns, severity of calculus accumulation and of alveolar resorption, occurrence of dental caries and/or abscesses and evidence for tooth loss *in vivo* or after burial.

The bones of the skeleton were examined for evidence of morphological anomalies, *ante mortem* damage, and disease. Extension of the range of measurements taken was found to be necessary in order to provide standards against which certain types of developmental upset could be assessed. Manifest skeletal adaptation (both metric and non-metric in character) was noted in order to monitor the evidence of environmental stress, whether chronic in nature (response to occupational, cultural or habitual strain, platymeria, platycnemia, degenerative change) or of acute form (trauma or healed injuries).[17] Similarly, evidence for chronic or acute disturbance of development was sought in growth abnormalities (measurable, intermittent or pathological) and in other forms of developmental hiatus (predisposition to response to increased stress as a result of congenital injury or nutritional disease).[18] Finally, skeletal evidence for pathology (other than dental pathology) present in the form of inflammation of bone as the result of reaction to the attack of disease organisms was noted.

Selections made from the data obtained were used to generate plans for the site, each graveyard plan focussing on a different aspect of the burials. The task was both simplified and accelerated by the use of a digital plotter in conjunction with a microprocessor.[19] The computer plots allowed rapid analysis of the variation of age at death across the burial ground and of other skeletal trends and traits. The results are discussed on page 48.

(b) Demography: the population

The data base consisted of 234 burials, supplemented by redeposited or otherwise unstratified human skeletal material from the site. The unstratified bones bear context numbers below 5000; redeposited material is so identified in the text when of pathological interest.

The 234 skeletons were looked upon initially as a single population despite certain difficulties with the skeletal evidence (which will be considered in due course). Half the burials were deficient in the head region and a mere 36 skeletons could be considered complete.

As so often, conventional procedures failed to permit the exhaustive sexing of the articulated skeletal remains. The current results presented here (Fig 30) include 19 adults for whom a confident opinion as to gender could not be expressed and they are therefore recorded here as 'unknown'. The population included 90 males

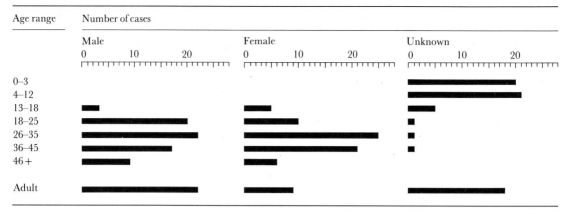

Age range	Number of cases								
	Male			Female			Unknown		
	0	10	20	0	10	20	0	10	20

30. Age at death and apparent mortality rate.

and 71 females, giving an adult sex distribution for the site of 1.27:1, respectively.[20]

Similar difficulties attended ageing of the burials. Chief among these problems was the fact that of the 180 adult burials many lacked the evidence necessary to assign the remains to the relevant age categories. At present, all that can be said of the 47 mature individuals of 'unknown' age is that they were fully adult (minimum 17 years old at the time of death). Since, however, the number of adults in the cemetery demonstrably over the age of 45 was small (15 individuals) it is likely that this 'unknown' category conceals persons belonging to this older age group.[21] Those shown to have exceeded the age of 45 occupied a mere 6.4% of the population. This represents 8.3% of the adult total or 11.3% of the adult remains capable of close age assessment. This is in sharp contrast with the medieval cemetery of St Helen-on-the-Walls, Aldwark, York, where 22–50% of the ageable adults fell within this age group, though markedly less so with British medieval series in general, where 9.9% of adults exceeded the age of 50 at death.[22]

The above discussion of ageing involves mature adults and excludes young adults (17 to 25 years of age) and sub-adults. The latter group was composed of adolescents (13 to 16 years old) and juveniles (comprising children of 3 to 12 years and infants of 2 years old or less). Once again there were problems with the juvenile category, the low proportion of neonates, infants and children skewing the population analysis. At a total of 41 individuals (or only 17.5% of the articulated burials) the proportion is lower than 30–50% expected for a pre-industrial society with low standards of hygiene and nutrition. Such short-

falls have precedents in other medieval cemeteries that have been excavated, however, and the explanations that have been offered are manifold.[23]

Subject to the above provisos further use was made of the demographic data obtained. Figs 5–11 show the distribution of the sexes and of the age of groups across the cemetery. In particular the demography of the burial types was considered. A slight preponderance of males over females was observed in Type I burials, whereas for the minor burial Types II, III and VI female interments were predominant. Type IV was equally distributed between the sexes and Type V consisted of a single infant.

(c) Continuous variation: the people

The average male stature was 5'8" (172.75 cm), with a range of 159.0 to 187.4 cm. Average height for females was 5'2" (157.50 cm) with a range of 150.0 to 173.7 cm. These figures are broadly consistent with the comparative series collected in Fig 31, as well as with the ranges for Britain in the present day.[24]

Many of the articulated skeletons were recovered without heads and of the remainder only a few (14 females and 8 males) were adequately preserved—with or without the need for reconstruction—to permit craniometry. Of these crania only 16 were sufficiently complete to allow determination of the cephalic index—a variable once used widely in anthropometry in the estimation of biological distance.[25] For the St Nicholas cemetery the skull type was *mesocephalic* (mean cranial index: 77.5; range: 70.4 to 87.4)

Site	Date	Heights		Sample size
		male	female	
Bidford-on-Avon	Saxon	5'7½" (171·45)	5'1½" (156·21)	large
North Elmham, Norfolk	,,	5'7¾" (172·09)	5'2" (157·62)	20
Porchester Castle	,,	5'9¼" (175·90)	5'5" (165·10)	15
St Helen, Aldwark, York	10th–16th	5'6½" (169·30)	5'2" (157·50)	large
Durham Cathedral	12th	5'7½" (171·45)	— —	20
Pontefract Priory	12th–14th	5'7½" (171·45)	— —	34
Wharram Percy DMV	medieval	5'6" (168·00)	— —	large
Greyfriars, Chester	,,	5'6½" (168·82)	5'3" (160·98)	20
Austin Friars, Leicester	,,	5'10" (177·80)	5'2" (157·50)	13
Bordesley Abbey	,,	5'8" (172·80)	— —	19
Rothwell Charnell House	,,	5'5" (165·10)	5'2" (157·60)	large
Dominican Priory, Chelmsford	,,	5'7" (170·18)	5'1½" (156·20)	25
Guildford Friary, Surrey	,,	5'8" (175·00)	5'3" (157·50)	56
St Mary's Priory, Thetford	12th–13th	5'9¾" (177·17)	— —	5
South Acre, Norfolk	12th–14th	5'6" (167·64)	5'1½" (156·21)	5
St Leonard's, Hythe, Kent	14th–15th	5'7" (170·2)	5'2" (157·40)	large
St Nicholas Shambles, London	11th–12th	5'8" (172·75)	5'2" (157.50)	94

31. *Mean stature (height in centimetres in parentheses) for Anglo-Saxon and English medieval populations.*[26]

and, overall, the vault was moderately low. The craniometric data are summarised in Fig 32, together with measurements determined for certain of the re-deposited skulls (5096, 5201).

The metrical results were of interest, chiefly because the mean cephalic index was not of extreme form. The majority of the St Nicholas crania lay between Anglo-Saxon or pre-Conquest dolichocephaly (3 skulls) and medieval brachycephaly (also 3 skulls), the latter being typified by material excavated from Winchester, Wharram Percy and York.[27]

In even fewer skulls from the site (13 crania) was the bony palate sufficiently intact for the standard measurements to be performed. However, the palatal index calculated (mean 119.3) was consistent with an early medieval population. On average the hard palate was short and broad, lacking any tendency for the crowding of teeth.[28]

Skeletal adaptation was explored quantitatively, both in the articulated burials and in the unstratified human remains. The measured antero-posterior and transverse diameters for the femur and tibia were used to calculate the meric

and cnemic indices, respectively.

The femur shaft index (platymeric index), based upon the ratio of the minimum antero-posterior diameter of the femur shaft, below the lesser trochanter to the transverse diameter at the same level for the thigh bones for 73 persons was 79.3. Platymeria (meric index 84.5) was observed in 56 femora: 78% overall (any difference between the sexes was not statistically significant). The preponderance of appropriate flattening of the upper one-third of the thigh bone is held in common with other early populations and has been attributed variously to habitual or nutritional factors.[29]

Determination of the cnemic index (a means of expressing the side-to-side flattening of the tibia, at the level of the nutrient foramen, based upon the ratio of the transverse diameter of the bone to its antero-posterior diameter) likewise involved certain inherent difficulties in interpretation.[30] However, the overall frequency of platycnemia (cnemic index 62.9) in 46 tibiae was 8.7%. This low level, taken with a *mean* cnemic index of 70.3 (range 51.2 to 85.7) is indicative of

Context number	Sex	Cranial Measurements (mm)											
		L	B	B'	S₁	S₂	S₃	S'₁	S'₂	S'₃	FL	FB	LB
5053	F				127			108					
5091	M		145			120	123		108	96			
5096	F	187	148	101	143	147	109	120	127	86			
5100	F	173			135	124	115	111	103	93			
5118	M		142	103		130	134		115	110			
5131	M	182	131						117				101
5147	F	190	151	97	132	131		109	109				
5157	F	175	141										
5158	F	179	135	100	117	130	115	104	115	90			
5189	F	184	142	100	128	118	132	108	104	105	34	32	99
5190	F	189	133										
5192	F			90	133			109					
5195	M	184	139										
5200	F	167	134	88	99	107	88	112	124	108	33	29	99
5201	F	181	144	100	107	113		123	138				
5202	F	171	149	101	118	108	124	101	98	98	36	30	95
5207	F	180	138	100	139	128	108	116	114	93	36	32	99
5213	M	179	138	91	124	119	128	105	106	99	33	29	97
5216	M					130							
5225	F			100	134	126		113	107				
5229	M	182	136	96	122	138	118	103	120	90	32	29	97
5236	M	197	150	102	134			113			41	31	101
5237	M	179	139										
5240	F					130	114		114	92			
1195A	F	191	150	97	127	114		111	104				
1195B	M	180	150	89	132	121	121	111	107	94	33	31	96
1195C	F	167	142	100	117	107	113	101	94	92			
1195F	M	191	148	97	127	133		110	117				
1253A	F	187	146	96	124	125	129	107	111	101	33	28	97
1323A	M	185	143	87	128	128	122	113	114	97			
1328A	F		150			129	110		106	95			
1334A	M	185	139	92	127			112					
1458A	M	186	140	90	131	127	133	107	114	104	33	28	95

32. *Craniometric data.*

H'	G'H	GL	GB	J	O'$_1$	O$_2$	NB	NH	SC	DC	Cephalic index	Context number
												5053
												5091
											79·1	5096
												5100
126												5118
											72·0	5131
											79·4	5147
106											80·6	5157
											75·4	5158
	68						23	52			77·1	5189
											70·4	5190
												5192
											75·5	5195
113	58	88			37	31	24	49	11		80·2	5200
											87·4	5201
											76·6	5202
119											76·6	5207
	67	91	86	121	37	31	26	48	11	21	77·1	5213
												5216
												5225
	67	98	89	126	36	33		50	8	22	74·7	5229
	75	93	88	139	38	34	24	57	12	26	76·1	5236
											77·7	5237
												5240
											77·1	1195A
									5	19	83·3	1195B
											85·0	1195C
	65	91	93		37	31	23	46	9	22	77·5	1195F
											78·1	1253A
											77·3	1323A
												1328A
											75·1	1334A
											75·3	1458A

a 'normal' population, in anthropological terms. The observed low rate for platycnemia is comparable to that for other English sites such as Anglo-Saxon Norfolk (7.1%), St Helen's, York (7.0%), or the Greyfriars, Chester (6.1%), and—as in the last of these—involved females only. This, then, may reflect a sex-specific habitual bone response.[31]

Here, as in other archaeological populations, no correlation between platymeria and platycnemia was observed. There was, moreover, no association with the so-called 'squatting facets' which, in this population, were entirely lacking.

(d) Discontinuous variation: the families

Discontinuous traits in the skeletons were monitored because of their bearing upon possible family relationships among the articulated burials, since regular departures from known frequencies are regarded as indicators of close kinship among the deceased. Analogous non-metric variation in the unstratified bones, although noted here, was of lower utility.

The traits involved are chiefly those of the skull and, although few crania remained intact, 117 were present in various states of fragmentation. Thus, amid the 234 burials any skeletal variable was recorded not as an overall frequency but rather as a proportion of the possible cases. Similarly the re-deposited crania were examined for congenital traits even though the potential kinship information was forfeit.

The cranial-variable frequencies for the articulated skeletons are summarised in Fig 33. The incidence of lambdoid wormian bones (43.6% of possible cases) is unexceptional since it appears that this anomaly was more common in earlier times than it is in the present day. Indeed, the data for English medieval sites cluster around a frequency of about 50% of skulls.[32] However, a phenomenon so widespread in the population could not be used, in isolation, in the elucidation of potential family relationships. The congruence of distinctively shaped wormian bones in two individuals would have been of greater value (as with the inca bones, below).

The figures for other sutural bones are also presented in Fig 33. The two skulls with bipartite inca bones were of persons who were possibly related. The frequencies of the maxillary *tori*—at about one to five per cent—were extremely low in comparison with medieval York.[33]

Trait	No. of possible cases	% of possible cases
Metopic suture	12/106	11·3
Lambdoid wormian bones	49/117	43·6
Sagittal sutural bones	4/117	3·4
Coronal sutural bones	8/117	6·8
Inca bones	5/117	4.3
Torus auditivus	1/117	0·9
Torus palatinus	6/117	5·4
Torus maxillaris	2/92	2·2
Torus mandibularis	0/107	0·0

33. Frequencies of non-metric variables of the skull.

A persistent metopic suture (or metope) was present in the skulls of 12 persons: 7 female, 4 male and 1 indeterminate. The frequency of metopism at the site (11.3%) may be compared with medieval York (11%), Hythe, Kent, (9%), 17th century Londoners (9%) and Anglo-Saxons (8.3%).[34] A high frequency of a cranial variable may be indicative of family relationship among those who share the same trait. The computed plot of the distribution of metopism in the cemetery (Fig 34) was one of several attempts to detect concentrations of burials suggestive of family groupings in the graveyard.

The likelihood of a family relationship must be greater when the metope is found in combination with other discontinuous traits. Thus, 5 skulls (4.7% of possible cases) were both metopic and showed wormian bones and of these 3 (2.8%) also displayed absence of the third molar. In these instances, as with the two cases of bipartite inca bones and three of a particularly prominent nose, the potential for close kinship is enhanced.

Among the articulated skeletons excavated, the jaws were substantially complete in 92 individuals (77 of them adult) and in a further 15 (13 adults) the dentition was represented by the lower jaw only. The dentition was often present, at least in the upper jaw, in redeposited skulls but no significant dental anomalies were noted.

Of the non-metric variables in the jaw that have a possible bearing upon family relationship is the failure of one or more of the third molars (or 'wisdom teeth') to develop. Third molar absence was noted in 30 dentitions (33% of possible cases), with a smaller incidence of reduced

34. Distribution of metopic suture in skeletons.

roots (4, ie 4.4%, all female)—such agenesis being expressed more frequently in the lower jaw, as at Clopton, Cambridge.[35] The trait concerned is encountered more often in females than in males but for St Nicholas Shambles the sexes were represented equally (14 each plus 2 of indeterminate sex). The overall frequency of third molar absence can be compared with other sites in Fig 35.

Sex	Tooth		No. failing to develop	No. possible in sample	% absent
	Upper M3	Left	6	28	21·4
		Right	4	27	14·8
M	Lower M3	Left	6	27	22·2
		Right	9	27	33·3
	Upper M3	Left	4	27	14·8
		Right	2	27	7·4
F	Lower M3	Left	5	28	17·8
		Right	6	28	21·4

35. Frequency of third molar absence in some English cemetery excavations.[36]

In those cases where all four quadrants of the dentition were available for study 52% had only one molar (M3) undeveloped, 44% had two, 4% had three but none had all four missing. The distribution of third molar agenesis by sex and region of dentition affected is given in Fig 36.

Site	Third molar agenesis (%)
St Nicholas Shambles, London	33·3
Mitre Street, London	33·3
Clopton, Cambridge	31·8
St Helen, York	22–26
Anglo-Saxon (pooled)	7·0

36. Third molar agenesis.

The only other expression of congenital dental absence in the population was that of the second premolar (P2). There were 3 cases (3.3%) of this form of hypodontia, in two of which it occurred in combination with third molar absence.

Hyperdontia (the occurrence of supernumerary teeth in the dentition) was rarer than hypodontia, affecting only 3 adults (3.3%) in total. In one of these individuals the extra tooth was expressed as an additional premolar in the upper right quadrant of the jaw, whereas in the other two cases it was a non-specific palatal tooth, occupying a position at the front of the mouth.[37]

Of the remaining discontinuous dental traits noted the 'shovelling' of the permanent incisor teeth was of great interest because this feature is an indication of kinship among those affected.[38] Shovel-shaped incisors appeared in 6 skulls (6.6% of the jaws studied) (for discussion see p.48).

Teeth with multiple roots were observable in certain individuals in whom post-mortem damage had loosened the teeth or had exposed their roots *in situ* in the jaw. In all, 5 examples of double-rooted canine teeth and one double-rooted upper central incisor were recorded.

Discontinuous traits in the post-cranial skeleton were less frequent. A trochlear foramen was present in the humerus in 20% of possible cases. It is a little-studied characteristic of uncertain significance and frequencies from 20–40% have been quoted.[39]

Two forms of anomaly of the sternum were noted, each occurring as a single case. There was a perforate gladiolus and segmentation of the body of the sternum in an adult (5068).[40]

There were several instances of the fusion of two cervical vertebrae (Fig 39). Such fusion tends to run in families.[41] Detachment of the neural arch was observed in an isolated lumbar vertebra amid the 234 articulated burials (the Anglo-Saxon frequency was as high as 8%).[42]

Primary aplasia of the hip appeared in three instances—all from among the unstratified bones. One of these was the left innominate bone of an adolescent girl (1125). In this specimen there was agenesis of the left pubic bone and the remaining bones of the hip on this side had united so that the acetabulum of the hip joint was not fully formed (Fig 38).

The unstratified material also included two cases of fusion of bones of the foot (in each of which both the calcaneus and talus were involved, Fig. 37). These specimens were not X-rayed and, therefore, a pathological cause for the fusion could not be ruled out. On the other hand, even if these cases were genuine examples of a congenital phenomenon, their unstratified source precluded their use in elucidating kinship group-

37. Fusion of calcaneus and talus (unstratified skeleton 'IC').

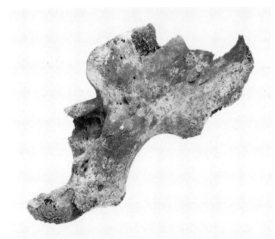

38. Hip aplasia (1125).

39. Fusion of cervical vertebrae (5158).

ing in the graveyard.

One of the articulated skeletons (5220) showed a severe congenital disorder affecting growth. The individual was a victim of diaphyseal aclasia, an hereditary defect in the development of the limb bones and which affects chiefly males (Fig 40).[43] This case serves to emphasize the importance of access to the entire skeleton for the diagnosis of disease, for a preliminary assessment of the condition (based, apparently, upon the examination of a solitary humerus from the skeleton) had been achondroplasia.[44] Although close inspection and measurement of the bones of this 30-year-old man suggested that he grew to be beneath average height for the population, he was far from being an achondroplastic dwarf.

Among the chronic ailments in the population was the single case of *coxa vara*, an orthopaedic disorder affecting the hip joint. A congenital predisposition during adolescence to the slipping of the head epiphysis of the femur had led to impairment of the right hip joint (Fig 41). The latter condition affects females, generally between the ages of 11 and 13, and usually the obese individual who was tall for her age (indeed, the individual concerned was taller than average for the site). What was observed in the remains of the 30-year-old woman was likely to have been the complication of an adolescent injury, untreatable at the time. This was to result in severe restriction of the mobility of the hip joint, extensive osteophytic growth surrounding the affected femoral head causing sympathetic eburnation of the corresponding acetabulum. The woman would have walked with a limp, the bones of the afflicted leg remaining more slender than those of the (increasingly) weight-bearing side, as the sound limb came to take on a greater share of load-bearing in response to the original injury.[45]

(e) Health and disease

An interesting finding concerning the articulated skeletons was the relative lack of pathological specimens. The state of health of the population may be discussed primarily in terms of the dental evidence and of age- or work-related conditions.

The available jaws (eg Fig 42) showed the full range of dental development from the eruption of the deciduous teeth, through adult dentition to severe attrition, pulp exposure and tooth loss. In almost all sets of jaws dental occlusion was such that the teeth made good contact and the upper

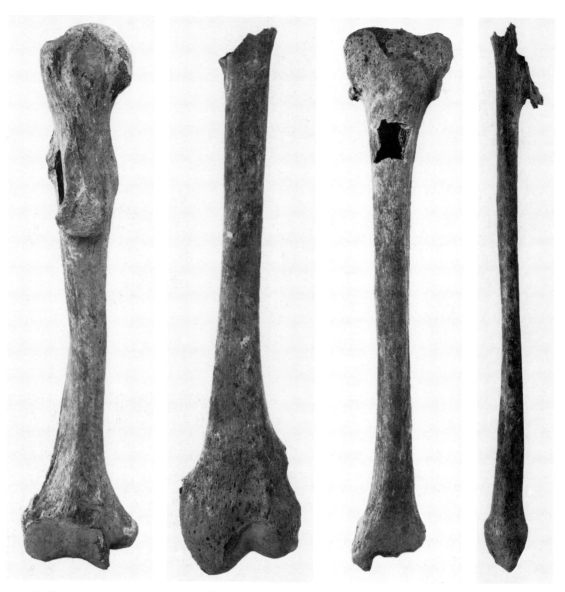

40. Diaphyseal aclasia (5220) : (a) humerus, (b) femur, (c) tibia, (d) fibula.

and lower front teeth met edge-to-edge (ie 'normal bite' rather than the prevalent modern condition of 'overbite'). This meant that, in addition to the rear teeth, the crowns of the incisors and canines frequently experienced severe wear also.

So far as general dental health was concerned 88.2% of jaws of immature persons showed no sign of disease (the balance were affected by dental caries). However, among the adult dentitions the proportion free of dental defects fell to a mere 12.2%.

The general state of oral hygiene in the population was indicated by the high degree of calculus deposited on the teeth. Dental calculus was found in 60% of all jaws (or in 75% of the adult dentitions). Moreover, in 45% of adult jaws the calculus deposit was of at least medium intensity, revealing both the absence in the population of the regular habit of detaching dental plaque from the teeth and the lack of any self-cleaning dietary practice.[46]

These calculus deposits presumably were one

41. *Coxa vara (5101)*.

42. *Dentition of skeleton 5118*.

of the causes of periodontal disease (a chronic condition of the gums and underlying bony alveolar tissue). Periodontal disease affected about half of the jaws, (46% overall, 56% of adults), and was distributed equally between the sexes. The incidence of apparent alveolar resorption was hence comparable to other medieval series studied on the continent of Europe (44 to 74%).[47]

Dental caries (tooth decay) was less common, being evident in only 40% of mouths, or less prevalent still if the overall proportion of teeth *at risk* was taken into account. Thus, only 5.5% of the teeth preserved showed evidence of caries. This figure appears low by English medieval standards (it is, for example, only half the Clopton frequency), although it is similar to the prevalence in Anglo-Saxon cemeteries (Fig 43).

A dental abscess (periapical osteitis—a possible sequel to dental caries) was seen in only 6 sets of jaws (6.6%)—a very low apparent sepsis rate. It is of interest here, however, that all those afflicted were over 35 years of age.[48] Chronic periapical infection can affect the dentition in quite another

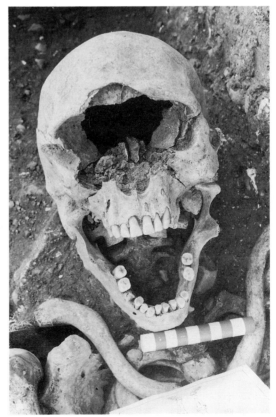

Site	Date	% Teeth with Caries
General	Anglo-Saxon	5·6
Porchester Castle	Saxon	5·1
North Elmham	Late Saxon	6·4
St Nicholas Shambles	11th–12th century	5·5
St Helen's Aldwark	10th–16th century	6·1
Clopton, Cambs.	medieval	11·1
Greyfriars, Chester	,,	9·0
Wharram Percy	,,	8·1

43. Dental caries rate for various English cemetery sites.[49]

way for it is sometimes associated with hypercementosis (nodule formation) of the tooth root.[50] This unusual feature appeared in 3 individuals (3.3%), all of whom had several molars affected (Fig 44).

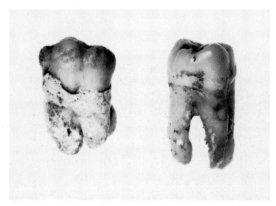

44. Hypercementosis (5070).

The loss of teeth during life was apparent in most dentitions. The overall frequency of *ante-mortem* tooth loss was 44.4% of jaws, or 7.6% of possible teeth. The type of tooth lost was chiefly molar. Analysis of tooth-loss prior to death, in the requisite sub-groups in the population, again showed little difference between the sexes. The observed shedding of a total of 145 teeth by the 40 sets of jaws involved a mean *ante-mortem* tooth-loss rate of 3.5 teeth per individual affected. The frequencies of tooth loss found here appear high by reference to Anglo-Saxon material but are consistent with skeletal remains of later date.[51]

A high frequency of tooth-loss in a medieval population is attributable not only to such afflic-

tions as dental caries and abscesses but to progressive loosening of the teeth in the jaw as the consequence of periodontal disease. The first two of these mechanisms for the loss of teeth during life, although common in later times, appear to have operated in smaller measure at the St Nicholas site than that involving infection of the gums and recession of the alveolar bone. In turn, the observed alveolar resorption in the jaws from the site may be the result of the continuous emergence of the teeth from the gum in response to the extreme attrition of their crowns or, equally, of a predisposition to destructive periostitis owing to the accumulation of calculus evident upon the surviving teeth. The overwhelming preponderance of molars and premolars lost *ante-mortem*, compared to front teeth, supports the above argument for tooth loss caused by periodontitis rather than as the result of dental caries.[52]

The final condition of a dental nature that was noted was *hypoplasia* (a defect of the development of the crowns of the teeth). It occurs when the development of the enamel of the tooth crown is interrupted by a serious illness, a vitamin deficiency or some metabolic disturbance of normal calcification. From knowledge of the age at which the tooth crowns involved are in course of formation in the gum it is possible to deduce the age(s) at which developmental interruption occurred. For the site concerned there are few cases of hypoplastic striations upon the crowns of molars or premolars the overwhelming majority occurring on canines and, especially, incisors (Fig 45). The crowns of these last two types of teeth are formed between the ages of 6 and 7 and between 4 and 5, respectively, suggesting that the illness or other form of metabolic upset peaked at these ages during the childhood of the affected per-

45. Extreme hypoplasia of tooth crown (5164).

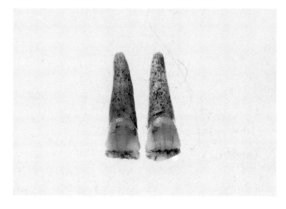

sons.[53] Interestingly, subject to the earlier reservations concerning the suspiciously small number of child burials, there appears to have been no excess of deaths in the narrow age-range deduced in the above argument. Thus, if a childhood illness is to be implicated as a cause of the enamel defects observed then it must have been one that was rarely fatal (non-specific childhood fevers, 'summer diarrhoea', etc).

If the alternative explanation for the phenomenon—vitamin D deficiency, possibly arising from malnutrition—were valid then one ought to have found frequent manifestations of this hypovitaminosis elsewhere in the skeleton.[54] Such rachitic modification of the long bones of the lower limbs has not been encountered regularly in the skeletal remains from the site. Finally, rickets is a disease that has yet to be recognised in English skeletal material of such an early date and is not to be expected during the 11th or 12th centuries with the presumed high incident sunshine in England appropriate to the time and with a diet thought to have been adequate in dairy products so as to supply the essential vitamin and calcium.[55]

A form of nutritional disease that did occur was that known as cribra orbitalia. This manifestation of osteoporosis was evident as a mild form of pitting in the bony orbit, although a minority of specimens had involvement of the femur (cribra femora) or the vault of the skull (parietal osteoporosis). The disease was present in 17% of skulls and, other than dental caries and hypoplasia, it was the only condition found that affected the immature persons in the site.

The porotic defect of bone manifested as cribra orbitalia has been observed in leprous skeletons but there is no evidence for leprosy in the target areas (jaws, hands, feet) of the skeletal remains from the St Nicholas site.[56] A lengthy review of the subject of *cribra* rejected many of the contributory causes suggested (malnutrition, deficiencies of vitamins A and D, etc) but implicated iron-deficiency anaemia as the chief agent. Furthermore, recent studies using documentary sources have suggested that owing to a diet that was deficient in iron, chronic anaemia was widespread in Europe during the middle ages and that

46. Cribra orbitalia (5129).

this dietary 'adverse iron budget' would have had more severe repercussions for the adult medieval female.[57] The findings from St Nicholas Shambles do not support this thesis, however, for there was no detectable excess of female sufferers over males. This is as expected for a condition such as cribra orbitalia which develops before puberty. It may be of greater significance that any disadvantages of a low-iron diet are aggravated by unhygienic conditions and, in particular, by parasitic infections as recent research concerning the link between childhood anaemia and cribra orbitalia has confirmed.[58] (Figs 46–7).

Turning to the post-cranial skeleton, osteoarthritis was found present as a degenerative disease affecting most of the joints, to some degree, but overwhelmingly the vertebral column. Overall at least 40% of the adults were affected (or 62.3% of possible cases). However, because of the uncertainty in ageing some of the adults the degenerative changes could not be analysed in terms of the narrow age-bands dealt with elsewhere. Although within the limited sample indicated the arthritic changes appeared more

marked in persons over the age of 25 (45.3% of possible cases affected) than in young adults (13.3%), evenly divided between the sexes, this is far from saying that the observed degeneration was as a direct result of the ageing process. Indeed, there is considerable evidence from other sites that osteoarthritic degeneration may be induced merely by stress or trauma. Some support for the latter mechanism comes from a consideration of the specific location in the spinal column of the observed osteophytic alterations. The overall incidence of degenerative change was identical in both complete and incomplete spines, (*viz.* 62.3%), yet there were very few examples of the former in which the entire spine was involved.

On the question of the specific region of the vertebral column involved, the ratio of such spondylitic changes seen in the cervical, thoracic or lumbar vertebrae was 2:4:3, respectively. That the vertebral involvement of the spine as a whole was non-uniform contests the traditional view in which such degenerative changes have been attributed to simple ageing. Hence, the apparent increase in prevalence with age need be

47. Parietal osteoporosis (5131).

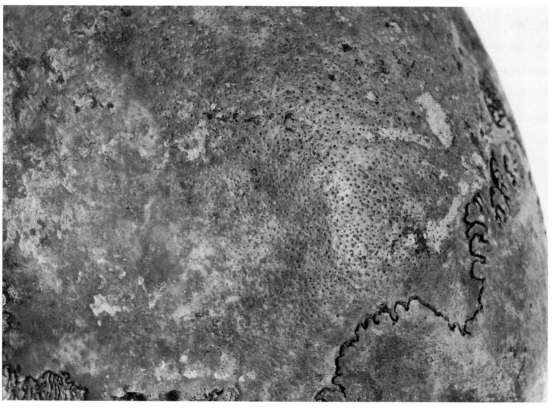

no more than a reflection of an increase in exposure to stress, trauma and simple wear-and-tear over a prolonged time.

Males and females were affected almost equally for each portion of the spinal column considered and, therefore, the observed spondylosis does not appear to reflect a sex-difference in habit or division of labour. However, one form of spinal degenerative disorder did seem to be sex-specific for the site, *viz.* Schmorl's nodes of the thoracic vertebrae. These marked impressions of the intervertebral disc were encountered in 8.6% of the thoracic spines preserved, males being afflicted four times as often as females. This observed sex-difference may represent a response to weight-bearing (the strain of heavy lifting?), perhaps occupational in origin.[59]

Of the large joints the hip was involved less frequently with osteoarthritic changes than the shoulder joint (and the peripheral joints still less so).[60] Here, again, these may have been the result of stress or of a traumatic predisposing cause. In the majority of cases (10) the degenerative change to the shoulder took the form of slight eburation of the distal end of the clavicle. The clavicle is one of the bones known to become modified as the result of manual labour and since in the St Nicholas cemetery male sufferers outnumbered females 9:1 this is further evidence for occupational disease at the site.[61]

There were few other types of pathological conditions affecting large numbers of persons from the site. An initial survey had indicated a high frequency of osteomyelitis and periostitis, or of Paget's disease, in the population but it is likely here that the much disturbed nature of the inhumations had led to this early confusion.[62] It is important to make a distinction between the articulated burials, (where an attempt could be made to assess the health of the individual as a whole), and selected pathological specimens among the unstratified bones. For example, inflammation of the periosteum of the long bones was the manifestation of pathology most widely encountered in the unstratified human skeletal remains, yet although specimens revealing periostitis were found among the articulated skeletons, as a proportion of the population as a whole the incidence was unremarkable. Similarly, Paget's disease (*osteitis deformans*) could not be confirmed at the site. Given the lack of elderly persons in the cemetry the absence of bone disease that afflicts predominantly those over 40 years of age is again unsurprising.

Turning now to the forms of cancer that may occur in bony tissue, bone tumours were few at the London site and none was malignant in

48. Osteoma (sinus knob) (arrowed) (5144).

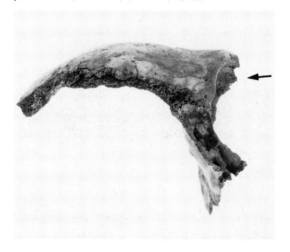

49. Destruction of head of humerus (5040).

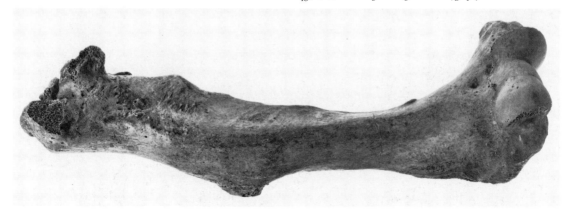

nature. Several skulls showed small benign osteomata, either single or multiple.[63] In a single instance the neoplasm was present not on the surface of the skull vault but within, as a 'sinus knob' (Fig 48).

The skeletal evidence for forms of infection was meagre. The rarity of periosteal inflammation, perhaps representing a secondary reaction (with soft-tissue infection following a wound to the limb) has been mentioned in passing. Specific infections were not evident at the site (and this includes the failure to observe tuberculosis in the skeletal remains).

Among individual illnesses, a distorted humerus initially had earned for another articulated skeleton perfunctory classification as an achondroplastic dwarf.[64] In fact, closer inspection of the skeleton of this individual showed that his other arm, though crushed after burial, was of normal dimensions (5040). The appearance of the affected right arm was such as to suggest that the epiphysis of the head of the humerus had been destroyed during childhood, (Fig 49).

Finally, the example of gallstone from one of the articulated burials (5306) ought to be considered. Such cases usually involve overweight adults in the fifth decade of life; and, indeed, this man was aged between 36 and 45 at the time of death.[65]

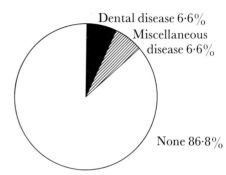

50. *Distribution of disease (%) in two groups of the population.*

(f) Injuries

Few wounds sustained during life were discernible. There were three cases of cranial injury. One skull (5047) showed evidence of a blow from an edged weapon, probably a sword. A blow struck from behind, presumably by a right-handed assailant, had removed a slice from the right frontal bone (Fig 51). The injury need not have proved fatal (for the injury was not to the full thickness of the cranium); however, the discrete edge of the wound showed no sign of having healed over and, therefore, the victim may not have survived for long after it was sustained.[66] One of the redeposited skulls had a penetrating wound caused by a missile and was probably fatal (5201). Yet another redeposited cranium (5096) showed a puncture wound (Fig 52).

Healed fractures were relatively uncommon. The intact bones of the lower limbs showed little evidence of trauma. There were 'greenstick' fractures to one femur and one tibia. Two further tibiae revealed healed fractures, one of them in conjunction with a broken fibula from the same leg. Trauma was more common in the upper limbs, particularly in the forearm. Thus, there was a healed Colles fracture of the distal end of the radius, a badly healed elbow joint and three other fractures of the arm involving both the radius and the ulna (Fig 53 and 54). There was a single fracture of the shoulder (left scapula) and two of the humerus, one of them also involving the clavicle. There were two other instances of fracture of the clavicle demonstrating the ease with which this bone may be broken by the force transmitted during a fall onto the outstretched hand. Fractured ribs appeared rare (3 possible examples).

The observed fracture rate appeared low by comparison with the Anglo-Saxons. It may reflect the advantages of urban life and, hence, of the higher risk activities of rural areas.[67]

Some of the foot bones showed deformities in addition to the arthritic changes. In two individuals the fifth metatarsal revealed an exaggerated lateral curvature, being bent outward

51. Sword wound(?) (5047).

from the foot through an angle of about 30°. It has been suggested that such bowing of the foot bones may be the result of the habitual wearing of shoes that are too tight.[68] Furthermore, there were two instances of abnormal articulation of the ankle joint and two examples of a bunion (*hallux valgus*). The latter, again, is a chronic deformation of the foot that arises frequently during adolescence, often caused by constricting footwear and of which there are known examples in the archaeological literature (Fig 55).[69]

An attempt was made also to estimate fertility for the population, making use of the technique involving examination for scars left on the pelvis during pregnancy and childbirth. Unfortunately, few pelves were preserved adequately for meaningful results to be obtained, irrespective of the published reservations concerning the applicability of the method described.[70]

The probable case of an obstetric death of a young woman and child from the cemetery has been described by Calvin Wells. Dr Wells deduced that not only was the mother smallish, but that she possessed certain 'android features',

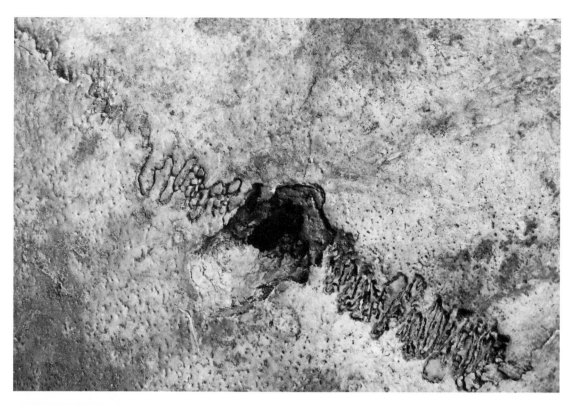

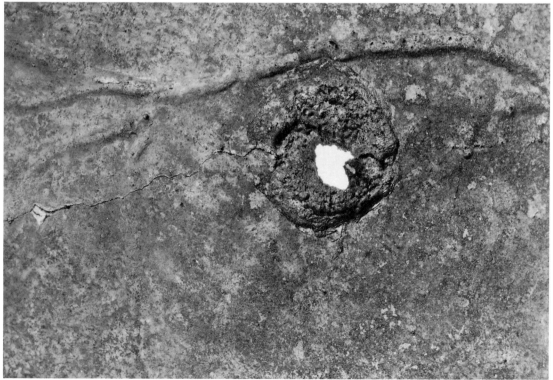

52. *Skull wound (5096): (a) exterior, (b) interior.*

53. Healed fracture of forearm (5218).

54. Trauma to forearm: joint disease and fusion (5198).

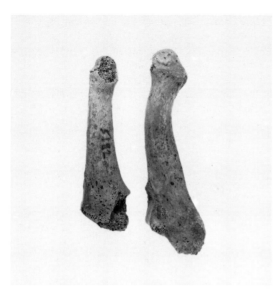

55. Distortion of 5th metatarsal (5307).

extending to a somewhat distorted pelvic cavity (5061).[71] His calculations suggested that the baby was a full term foetus of very large size with an unusually broad head (5062). Thus, he concluded that these features of her offspring were incompatible with the woman's inadequate pelvic canal and had led to the death of both of them during labour as the result of 'maternal exhaustion' (Appendix 3; and Figs 57–8).

(g) General population characteristics: life, health, culture and mortality

The 234 burials were analysed for social organisation using computer graphics but much of the evidence was negative. There did not appear to be a favoured location for the burial of children as has been encountered at other sites (notably Clopton, the Hirsel and Raunds) although a concentration of neonates and young children with adults at the south-western limit of the excavated area and at a second, minor part of the site could be suggestive of the burial of children with their parents.[72]

Analysis of the cemetery for possible family groupings of burials using non-metric traits of the skull produced some positive results. Thus, there was a concentration of burials in which the interments revealed the simultaneous shared characteristics of metopism, wormian bones and the absence of wisdom teeth.

In the analysis of burial types non-metric variation proved of greater utility that simple demography (there being no obvious age/sex distribution discernible in the cemetery). Thus, in the simple burials in the graveyard soil three individuals furnished with a pebble in the mouth all shared the traits of wormian bones in combination with the congenital absence of wisdom teeth (5192, 5195, 5240).

Trial plots of burials showing non-metric variations were not uniformly rewarding. Although the plot of metopic suture distribution in the cemetery had produced negative results (Fig 34, above) two adjacent burials shared the simultaneous characteristics of a pattern of discontinuous traits (metopic suture, wormian bones and third-molar absence) strongly suggesting that these two were closely related (5070, 5144). There were further examples of two non-metric traits found in common in certain skulls and hence possibly indicative of family relationships among those who showed these traits. When the combinant non-metric variables were plotted on the plan of the cemetery, however, unequivocal clustering of burials suggesting family groupings was not evident (Fig 56). Greater success attended the plotting of the burials that shared the non-metric cranial feature of shovelling of the incisor teeth. The trait was an indicator of close kinship among those at the site who showed its presence and this is expressed in Fig 56.

Anthropometry has been used in other studies in the estimation of biological distance in races and in smaller population groups.[73] Despite the disturbed nature of the site some general comments concerning the St Nicholas Shambles cemetery are possible.

The evidence from continuous and, especially, discontinuous variation was that males and females were from an homogeneous population such that there was little exogamy, brides apparently being selected from within London (if not from the same parish) and that there was little outward movement.[74] Thus, the meagre data suggest that the population during the period concerned were possessed of short, broad faces with medium-to-wide quadrate eye sockets. Noses were not particularly broad although a minority were prominent. Several of the crania showed a marked 'double crown': the two bulging parietals being separated by a deep sagittal depression.

The latter characteristics of the skull were quite distinct from the overall shape of the head which, as discussed above, revealed a departure from the long-headedness typical of Anglo-Saxons and fitted into the scheme of a tendency toward round-headedness during the medieval period. Two skulls exhibiting dolichocephaly were found buried appropriately adjacent to the early church structure (5131, 5229). They occur in the computer plot, along with a cluster of skulls showing brachycephaly (Fig 56). A transitional position for the population of the site appears to be confirmed by other features of the skeleton. In certain respects the properties of the skeletal remains resembled closely those known for Anglo-Saxon sites, whereas certain other aspects of the skeleton agreed more closely with cemetery populations of later date.

The human skeletal remains analysed for the site gave a coarse life span for the defined sample (assuming that the adults of 'unknown' age populated their lowest possible category: 17 to 25 years of age) of 30 years. This figure is rather low by comparison with contemporary Winchester and, especially, with later medieval London.[75]

By reference to other archaeological sites a high child-mortality rate is to be presumed. Nonetheless, of 193 persons who survived childhood 180 adolescents went on to become adults and, of these, 145 lived beyond the age of 25.

The apparent dearth of pathology observed ought not to be taken to imply that the population as a whole was particularly healthy, but merely that the ailments suffered were generally such as did not leave obvious traces upon the bones. On the contrary, the high incidence of dental hypoplasia and the low apparent age at death argue that the health of the public, in general, was greatly inferior to that in the same City of the present day.

The evidence concerning dental health was conflicting. The combined effect of diet and tooth occlusion was such as to cause severe attrition, (even in the front teeth of the young). However, since dental caries is causally linked with the consumption of refined carbohydrates, and since sugar, the worst offender, was not imported into England until the 12th century (or later still to London) the frequency of caries observed was close to the Anglo-Saxon minimum figure.[76] 'Normal bite' and the coarse, low calorific fare evidently available produced the profound attrition of the teeth observed and the formation of secondary dentine, while allowing ready deposition of calculus with eventual alveolar retraction and loss of teeth.[77]

Further evidence for chronic ill-health in the population comes in the form of the lesions of porotic hyperostosis (chiefly of cribra orbitalia). This may have had a bearing upon the standard of hygiene prevailing in the town because the anaemia with which the observed phenomenon is associated may be aggravated by poor hygiene. Indeed, later City ordinances complain of the nuisance caused by the disposal of domestic and industrial refuse in the street of what had become the butchering quarter of the City. Poor hygiene, too, would have promoted infestation by parasites such as the worms which have been implicated in iron-deficiency anaemia.

The low occurrence of healed fractures in the bones is of interest in that it may represent one of the advantages of urban life over rural occupations, as discussed above. The low frequency of wounds encountered is unsurprising if one accepts William Fitzstephen's description of the congenial disposition of Londoners at about this time: 'In this Place, the Calmness of the Air doth mollify men's minds, not corrupting them with Lusts, but preserving them from savage and rude Behaviour, and seasoning their Inclinations with a more kind and free Temper'.[78]

Certainly, the citizens appeared to be as much at risk from the whim of fashion as from the hand of man, deformities of the toes apparently being caused by the wearing of tight shoes. These latter perhaps were of the long, narrow, pointed variety numbered among the scandals prevailing at the court of William II in the 11th century, according to the chroniclers William of Malmesbury and Orderic Vitalis.[79]

Osteoarthritis, where it occurred, was not necessarily a feature of ageing. Indeed, since the type and incidence of the degenerative changes differed between the sexes, an occupational cause may have been involved. Similar sex-differences in certain forms of skeletal adaptation, discussed earlier, tended to confirm a division of labour between the sexes and to reveal diseases that were probably occupational in origin.

There were, however, a significant number of persons unable to participate equitably in the work-load of the community. The disabled sector of the population included those who had survived into adolescence, or beyond, with severe congenital disabilities, acute injuries or badly healed limb fractures. The evidence, therefore, is that their able-bodied fellows were both tolerant and supportive of this unfortunate minority—as is to be expected of a close-knit, Christian society.[80]

56. Burial alignments: burials showing special traits:
● *Shovelling* ▶ *Brachycephalic skulls* ◆ *Dolichocephalic skulls* ● *Combination of non-metric variables.*

AUTHOR'S ACKNOWLEDGEMENT

I am very grateful to Theya Molleson and Barbara West for reading and commenting upon an earlier draft of the text. Thanks are due also to Merry Morgan Hill for her part in the valuable recording of the skeletons *in situ* and, in consultation with Rosemary Powers, for the preliminary screening of the burials for evidence of pathology.

PUBLISHER'S ACKNOWLEDGEMENTS

The photographs in this book are work of Trevor Hurst, Jon Bailey, Jenny Orsmond, Jan Scriver, and Maggie Cox; the drawings are by Richard Lea. For the translations of the abstract I thank Dominique Vaughan and Frederike Hammer.

Footnotes and references

1. The material of choice is UHU All-Purpose Clear Adhesive. This adhesive does not discolour the bone specimen. Its further advantages are that the join produced is stable under the normal conditions of storage yet that bonding is reversible upon the application of a suitable solvent (eg acetone). Information kindly supplied by Miss Theya Molleson of the British Museum (Natural History), Sub-Department of Anthropology.

2. M. Morgan, 'Excavation and recording techniques used at the cemetery of St Nicholas Shambles, London' *London Archaeol* 3 (1978) 213–16.

3. N. Reynolds, 'The structure of Anglo-Saxon graves' *Antiquity* 50 (1976) 140–4.

4. S. Genovés, 'Sex determination in earlier man' in D.R. Brothwell and E. Higgs (eds), *Science in Archaeology: a Survey of Progress and Research* 2nd edition (1969) 429–39; S. Genovés, 'Estimation of age and mortality' *ibid.* 440–52; W.M. Bass 'Developments in the identification of human skeletal material (1968–1978) *AJPA* 51 (1979) 555–62; T.D. Stewart, 'Identification by the skeletal structures' in F.E. Camps (ed), *Gradwohl's Legal Medicine* 3rd edition (1976) 109–35; D.H. Ubelaker, *Human Skeletal Remains: Excavation, Analysis and Interpretation* (1978) 41–67; Workshop of European Anthropologists, 'Recommendations for age and sex diagnoses of skeletons' *J Hum Evol* 9 (1980) 517–49; D.R. Brothwell, *Digging Up Bones: the Excavation, Treatment and Study of Human Skeletal Remains* 3rd edition (1981) 59–72 and references therein.

5. S. Genovés, *op. cit.* 435–6; M.L. Moss, 'Analysis of developmental processes possibly related to human sexual dimorphism' in P.M. Butler and K.A. Joysey (eds), *Development, Function and Evolution of Teeth* (1978) 135–47; D.L. Anderson, 'Estimation of age, sex and body size in a mandible' *Ontario Dentist* 55 (1978) 9–10.

6. J.D. Dawes, 'The human bones' in J.D. Dawes and J.R. Magilton, *The Cemetery of St Helen-on-the-Walls,* *Aldwark* (1980) 23. The danger is that an elderly female skeleton might be mis-diagnosed as male on the basis of the rugged or corrugated appearance of certain bones with the concomitant under-representation of females in the graveyard analysis: T. Molleson, 'The archaeology and anthropology of death: what the bones tell us' in S.C. Humphreys and H. King (eds), *Mortality and Immortality: the Archaeology and Anthropology of Death* (1981) 15–31.

7. F.E. Camps and J.M. Cameron, *Practical Forensic Medicine* (1981) 119: D.R. Brothwell *Digging Up Bones* 62.

8. D.H. Goose, 'Dental measurement: an assessment of its value in anthropological studies' in D.R. Brothwell (ed), *Dental Anthropology* (1963) 125–48; S.M. Garn, A.B. Lewis, D.R. Swindler and R.S. Kerewsky, 'Genetic control of sexual dimorphism in tooth size' *J Dental Research* 46 (1967) 963; G.W. Thompson, D.L. Anderson and F. Popovich, 'Sexual dimorphism in dentine mineralisation' *Growth* 39 (1975) 289–301; Anderson, *op. cit.* n5, 9. For the mandibular canines from the St Nicholas site the distribution of crown diameters was: male > 7 mm, female < 7 mm.

9. I. Lengyel, 'Biochemical aspects of early skeletons' in D.R. Brothwell (ed) *The Skeletal Biology of Earlier Human Populations* (1968) 271–86; I. Kiszely, 'On the possibilities and methods of the chemical determination of sex from bones' *Ossa* 1 (1974) 51–62; J. Dennison, 'Citrate estimation as a means of determining the sex of human skeletal material' *Archaeology and Anthropology in Oceania* 14 (1979) 136–43; D.R. Brothwell, *Digging Up Bones* 59.

10. M.M. Maresh, 'Growth of major long bones in healthy children' *American Journal of Diseases in Children* 66 (1943) 227–54, 'Linear growth of long bones of extremities from infancy through adolescence' *ibid.* 89 (1955) 725–42; F.E. Johnson, 'Growth of the long bones in infants and children at Indian Knoll' *AJPA* 20 (1962) 249–54; P. M.

Gindhart, 'Growth standards for the tibia and radius in children aged one month through eighteen years' *ibid.* 39 (1973) 41–8; M. Stloukal and H. Hanakova, 'Die Länge der Längsknochen altslawischer Bevölkerungen unter besonderer Berücksichtigung von Wachtumsfragen' *Homo* 29 (1978) 53–69; R.J. Sundick, 'Human skeletal growth and age determination' *ibid.* 29 (1978) 228–49; J.M. Hoffman, 'Age estimations from diaphyseal lengths: two months to twelve years' *J Forensic Medicine* 24 (1979) 461–9; Ubelaker, *op. cit.* n4, 48–52; Dawes, *op. cit.* n6, 23–4, 62.

11. The requirements for a scheme for ageing skeletons based upon the calibration of wear upon the molar teeth is given in A.E.W. Miles, 'The dentition in the assessment of individual age of skeletal material' in D.R. Brothwell, *Dental Anthropology* 191–209. The ever-present risk of under-ageing of human skeletal remains has been emphasised by Theya Molleson (*op. cit.* n6, 20–21).

12. D.R. Brothwell, *Digging Up Bones* 73; D.D. Thompson, 'The core technique in the determination of age at death in skeletons' *J For Sci* 24 (1979) 902–915; 'Microscopic determination of age at death in an autopsy series' *ibid.* 26 (1981) 470–5; C.B. Ruff and W.C. Hayes, 'Subperiosteal expansion and cortical remodelling of the human femur and tibia with aging' *Science* 217 (1982) 945–8; S.D. Stout and S.J. Gehlert, 'The relative accuracy and reliability of histological ageing methods' *Forensic Science International* 15 (1980) 181–90.

13. D.R. Brothwell, *Digging Up Bones* 77–87; Dawes, *op. cit.* n6, 21–2.

14. M. Trotter and G.C. Gleser, 'Estimation of stature from long bones of American whites and negroes' *AJPA* 10 (1952) 436–514; 'A re-evaluation of estimation of stature based upon measurements of stature taken during life and long bones after death' *ibid.* 16 (1958) 79–123.

15. J.D. Dawes, *op. cit.* n6, 24.

16. D.R. Brothwell, *Digging Up Bones* 51–4.

17. J.D. Dawes, *op. cit.* n6, 55; R. Chapman and K. Randsborg, 'Approaches to the archaeology of death' in R. Chapman, I. Kinnes and K. Randsborg (eds) *The Archaeology of Death* (1981) 1–24 (22–3).

18. J.D. Dawes, *op. cit.* n6, 57; M. Harman, T. Molleson and J.L. Price, 'Burials, bodies and beheadings in Romano-British and Anglo-Saxon cemeteries' *Bull Brit Mus (Natur Hist) Geol* 35 (1981) 145–88 (153).

19. B. Alvey and J. Moffett, 'Hard copy graphic displays for archaeologists' *London Archaeol* 5 (1985) 40–6.

20. *cf.* Anglo-Saxon Raunds: A. Boddington, forthcoming report.

21. The ready comminution and destruction of the skeletons of the elderly is dealt with in R.J. Sundick, *op. cit.* n10, 231–2.

22. J.D. Dawes, *op. cit.* n6, 34–6; D.R. Brothwell, 'Palaeodemography and earlier British populations' *World Archaeol* 4 (1972) 75–87.

23. T. Molleson, *op. cit.* n6, 20–1; S. Genovés, *op. cit.* n4, 441 (quoting Howells); J.C. Russell, *British Medieval Population* (1948), 208–14, 'Recent advances in medieval demography' *Speculum* 40 (1965) 84–101 and references therein, especially: N-G. Gejvall, *Westerhus: Medieval Population and Church in the Light of Skeletal Remains* (1960) 35; T.H. Hollingsworth, 'A demographic study of the English ducal families' *Population Studies* 11 (1957) 4–26. Further data upon juvenile deaths in Anglo-Saxon Norfolk and Saxon/medieval Northumbria are collected in C. Wells, 'The human burials' in A. McWhirr (ed), *Cirencester Excavations II: Romano-British Cemeteries in Cirencester* (1982) 136.

Thus, the shallow nature of infant interments permit disturbance of such remains during subsequent inhuming, or other activities upon the site; J.D. Dawes, *op. cit.* n6, 27. These shallow infant burials may be subject further to losses through soil erosion or through the attentions of burrowing animals, although burial in a protective environment (such as within the church building itself) is no guarantee of the preservation of immature skeletal remains. Here the relative chemical lability of under-calcified tissue may be of significance; W. Rodwell, *The Archaeology of the English Church: the Study of Historic Churches and Graveyards* (1981) 148–9. That there is anything inherently unstable in buried infant skeletons has been disputed, however; R.J. Sundick, *op. cit.* n10, 232.

24. Average heights for modern Britons: male 5′8½″(173.8 cm), female 5′3½″(160.9 cm), Office of Population Census and Surveys, 'Adult Heights and Weights Survey' *OPCS Monitor*, SS 81/1 (1981).

25. Data obtained from: J.C. Brash, 'The Anglo-Saxon cemetery at Bidford-on-Avon, Warwickshire—Notes on the cranial and other skeletal characteristics' *Archaeologia*, 73 (1923) 106–10; C. Wells, 'Excavations at North Elmham Park, 1967–1972, 12: The human bones' *E Anglian Archaeol* 9 (1980) 247–374; B. Hooper, 'The Saxon burials' in B. Cunliffe (ed) *Excavations at Porchester Castle, Volume II: Saxon* (1976) 235–61; J.D. Dawes, *op. cit.* n6, 28–29; J.T. Fowler, 'The Chapter House of Durham Cathedral' *Archaeologia*, 45 (1880), 385–400; J.G.Hurst, 'Excavations at Pontefract Priory, Appendix G: coffins and interments' in C.V. Bellamy, *Pontefract Priory Excavations, 1957–61*, Publications of the Thoresby Society 49 (1965) 127–32; D.R. Brothwell, 'The Wharram Percy skeletons' in M. Beresford and J.G. Hurst, *Deserted Medieval Villa-*

ges (1971) 135; B.A. West, 'The human bones from the mediaeval Greyfriars site, Chester (1980, unpublished); A. Stirland, 'The human bones' in J.E. Mellor and T. Pearce, *The Austin Friars, Leicester* CBA Research Report No.35 (1981) 168–9 and microfiche 1 of 2; P.A. Rahtz and S. Hurst, 'Bordesley Abbey, First Report on Excavations 1969–1973' *Brit Archaeol Rep* 23 (1976) 116–7; C. Wells, 'The mediaeval burials' in R. Robertson-Mackay, 'Recent excavations at the Cluniac Priory of St Mary, Thetford, Norfolk' *Medieval Archaeol*, 1 (1957) Appendix A 99–103; C. Wells, 'A leper cemetery at South Acre, Norfolk' *ibid.* 11 (1967) 242–8; F.G. Parsons, 'Report on the Rothwell crania' *Journal of the Royal Anthropological Institute*, 40 (1910) 483–504; J. Bayley, 'Chelmsford Dominican Priory: human bone report' *Ancient Monuments Laboratory*, Report No.1890 (1975, unpublished); J.G.Parsons, 'Report on the Hythe crania' *Journal of the Royal Anthropological Institute*, 38 (1908) 419–50; J. Henderson, 'The human remains' in R. Poulton and H. Woods, *Excavations on the Site of the Dominican Friary at Guildford in 1974 and 1978* (1984) 58–67.

26. D.R. Brothwell, 'Microevolution in Man' *Science Journal*, 1 (1965) 79–85; *Digging Up Bones*, 87 and *op. cit.* n22, 82.

27. See graph in D.R. Brothwell, *Digging Up Bones* 2nd ed (1972), 92, (note that this material has been omitted from the same author's 3rd edition, *idem.*, *op. cit.* n4; on the other hand, see his discussion in *idem.*, *op. cit.* n22, 82 and in Beresford and Hurst, *op. cit.* n26, 135. The five medieval sites considered above (Abingdon, Hythe, Rothwell, Wharram Percy and Winchester) provide cranial indices which show that the population was *brachycephalic*, in sharp contrast to the evidence of Anglo-Saxon cemeteries wherein *dolichocephaly* prevailed (e.g. mean cephalic index 73, in Brash, *op. cit.* n25, 108). For the extensively excavated graveyard site at York, the claim has been made that the cephalic index determinations made upon the St Helen's, Aldwark, skulls '. . . demonstrate conclusively the change in mean within the city itself.', D.M. Palliser, 'Historical Assessment', in J.D. Dawes and J.R. Magilton, *op. cit.* n6, 82–3. However, this state of affairs for the city of York does not appear to be borne out by the published data which tend to show that this medieval population was 'largely brachycephalic', J.D. Dawes, *op. cit.* n6, 27 and Table 4, 30–31; see also *idem.* pers comm quoted in P.C. Buckland, 'Archaeology and Environment in York' *J Archaeol Sci*, 1 (1974) 303–16.

28. D.H. Goose, 'Reduction of Palate Size in Modern Populations' *Archives of Oral Biology*, 7 (1962) 343–50. The adequacy of jaw dimensions and the relative importance of tooth crowding, impaction and malocclusion are discussed in D.R. Brothwell, *op. cit.* n8, 79–80. Typically, the jaws of Anglo-Saxons have broad tooth arches, with minor crowding of the teeth: A.E.W. Miles, 'The Dentition of the Anglo-Saxons' *Proc Roy Soc Med*, 62 (1969) 1311–15; D.H. Goose and S.E. Parry, 'Palate Width in Skulls from a Recently Excavated English Mediaeval Site' *Archives of Oral Biology*, 19 (1974) 273–4; S.A. Frake and D.H. Goose, 'A Companion Between Mediaeval and Modern British Mandibles' *ibid.* 22 (1977) 55–7.

29. C. Wells, *Bones, Bodies and Disease: Evidence of Disease and Abnormality in Early Man* (1964) 132; D.R. Brothwell, *Digging Up Bones* 88; Dawes, *op. cit.* n6, 29.

30. D.R.Brothwell, *Digging Up Bones* 89–90; C. Wells, *op. cit.* n29 132–4; S. Andermann, 'The cnemic index: a critique' *AJPA* 44 (1976) 369–70; C.C. Lovejoy, A.H. Burstein and K.G. Heiple, ' The biochemical analysis of bone strength: a method and its application to platycnemia' *ibid.* 44 (1976) 489–506.

31. C.C. Lovejoy, A.H. Burstein and K.G. Heiple, *op. cit.* n30, 504. For York see J.D. Dawes, *op. cit.* n6, 29–30; for North Elmham and Chester see n25 above.

32. J.D. Dawes, *op. cit.* n6, 59; D.R. Brothwell, *Digging Up Bones* 92 Table 4. Similarly, the frequency of wormian bones observed at Hythe, Kent, was 50%: B.M. Stoessiger and G.M. Morant, 'A study of the crania in the vaulted ambulatory of St Leonard's church, Hythe' *Biometrika* 24 (1934) 135–202 (174).

33. J.D. Dawes, *op. cit.* n6, 60.

34. For York *see* J.D. Dawes, n6, for Hythe *see* Parsons, *op. cit.* n25, 434; for other sites, D.R. Brothwell, *Digging Up Bones* 92 Table 4.

35. I. Tattersall, 'The dental palaeopathology of mediaeval Britain' *J Hist Med 23* (1968) 380–5.

36. *Ibid.* 385; J.D. Dawes, *op. cit.* n6, 51; D.R.Brothwell, V.M. Carbonell and D.H. Goose, 'Congenital absence of teeth in human populations' in D.R. Brothwell, *Dental Anthropology* 179–90.

37. *cf.* D.R. Brothwell, *Digging Up Bones* 112 Fig 4.19 E.

38. V.M. Carbonell, 'Variations in the frequency of shovel-shaped incisors in different populations' in D.R. Brothwell, *Dental Anthropology* 211–34; V. Alexandersen, 'Double-rooted human lower canine teeth' *ibid.* 235–41; A.C. Berry, 'Anthropological and family studies on minor variants of the dental crown' in Butler and Joysey, *op. cit.* n5, 81–98.

39. D.R. Brothwell, *Digging Up Bones* 97. Data for a few British sites are collected in Wells, *op. cit.* n23, 142 Table 51.

40. S. Živanovič, *Ancient Diseases: the Elements of Palaeopathology* (1982) 98. This specimen (now unfortunately unavailable for study) was comparable to the Egyptian example illustrated in D.R. Brothwell, *Digging Up Bones* 171–2 Fig 6.20 C,D.

41. D.R.Brothwell and R. Powers, 'Congenital malformations of the skeleton' in D.R. Brothwell, *op. cit.* n9, 173–203.

42. *Ibid.* 198 Table IV.

43. *Ibid.* 182. Further possible examples, three in number, were said to have been seen among the unstratified bones from the St Nicholas site (information supplied by Maria Mabee).

44. S. Živanovič, *op. cit.* n40, 126.

45. S. Hughes, 'Common orthopaedic disorders' *Update: a Journal of Postgraduate General Practice* 24 (1982), 1919–30; D.R. Brothwell and R. Powers, *op. cit.* n41, 188–9; C. Wells, 'Abnormality in a mediaeval femur' *Brit Med J* 1 (1971), 504–5; F.H. Gibson, 'Genu recurvatum in association with slipped capital femoral epiphysis' *J Roy Soc Med* 74 (1981) 626–7.

46. V. Alexandersen, 'The pathology of the jaws and the temporomandibular joint' in D.R. Brothwell and A.T. Sandison (eds) *Diseases in Antiquity* (1967) 551–75; D.R. Brothwell, *Digging Up Bones* 155–60; C. Wells, *op. cit.* n23 150.

47. V. Alexandersen, *op. cit.* 567.

48. W.J. Moore and E. Corbett, 'The distribution of dental caries in ancient British populations: I. Anglo-Saxon period' *Caries Research* 5 (1971) 151–68; 'II. Iron-Age, Romano-British and Mediaeval Periods' *ibid.* 7 (1973) 139–53; S.W. Hillson, 'Diet and dental disease' *World Archaeol* 11 (1979) 147–61. Abscess frequencies (expressed as a percentage of tooth sockets) ranging from 2.73 (Anglo-Saxon) to 9.19 (medieval, Clopton) are given in I. Tattersall, *op. cit.* n35, 383.

49. D.R. Brothwell, 'Teeth in earlier populations' *Proceedings of the Nutrition Society* 18 (1959) 59–65; G.T. Emery, 'Dental pathology and archaeology' *Antiquity* 37 (1963) 274–81; C. Wells, *op. cit.* n23 148; Beresford and Hurst, *op. cit.* n25, 135; J.D. Dawes, *op. cit.* n6, 52; Tattersall, *op. cit.* n35, 381.

50. S.N. Bhaskar, *Orban's Oral Histology and Embryology* (1976) 199.

51. G.T. Emery, *op. cit.* n48, 277–8; D.R. Brothwell, *Digging Up Bones* 154–5. Paradoxically, although dental calculus may be one of the underlying causes of periodontalism it may, conversely, provide also a degree of protection against dental caries: *ibid.* 159–60.

52. *Ibid.* 154; H.N. Newman and B.G.H. Levers,

'Tooth eruption and function in an early Anglo-Saxon population' *J Roy Soc Med* 72 341–50; I. Tattersall, *op. cit.* n35, 382.

53. *cf.* D.C. Cook, 'Mortality, age-structure and status in the interpretation of stress indicators in prehistoric skeletons: a dental example from the Lower Illinois Valley' in Chapman, Kinnes and Randsborg, *op. cit.* n17, 133–44; G.T. Emery, 'Dental Archaeology' *Sci and Archaeol* 1 (1970) 12–14; P.D. Schultz and H.M. McHenry, 'Age distribution of enamel hypoplasia in prehistoric California indians' *J Dental Research* 54 (1975) 913; G.C. van Beek, *Dental Morphology: an Illustrated Guide* (1983) 2nd ed 126.

54. D.R. Brothwell, *Digging Up Bones* 159; A.H. Goodman and G.J. Armelagos, 'Factors affecting distribution of enamel hypoplasia within human permanent dentition' *AJPA* 68 (1985) 479–93.

55. D.R. Brothwell, *Digging Up Bones* 163–4; C. Wells, *op. cit.* n29 116–17; Buckland, *op. cit.* n27, 312.

56. C. Wells, *op. cit.* n25, 243.

57. O.P. Hengen, 'Cribra orbitalia: pathogenesis and probable etiology' *Homo* 22 (1971) 57–72; Chapman and Randsborg, *op. cit.* n17, 22; C. Wells, *op. cit.* n23, 186; V. Bullough and C. Campbell, 'Female longevity and diet in the middle ages' *Speculum* 55 (1980) 317–25.

58. O.P. Hengen, *op. cit.* 68–70; P.S. McAdam, 'Porotic hyperostosis: representation of a childhood condition' *AJPA* 66 (1985) 391–8.

59. D.R. Brothwell, *Digging Up Bones* 146; C. Wells, *op. cit.* n29, 60; Hooper, *op. cit.* n25, 238; C. Wells, *op. cit.* n23, 154–6; I. Swedborg, 'Studies of macerated human spine: a background for the clinical approach to the degenerative process' *Ossa* 2 (1975) 15–21.

60. *cf.* J. Rogers, I. Watt and P. Dieppe, 'Arthritis in Saxon and mediaeval skeletons' *Brit Med J* 283 (1981) 1668–70. The sites commonly affected in modern populations are summarised in E.C. Huskisson *et. al*, 'Another look at arthritis' *Annals of Rheumatic Disease* 38 (1979) 423–9.

61. T.B. Johnston, D.V. Davies and F. Davies (eds), *Gray's Anatomy* (1958) 358; L. Wilkinson, 'problems of analysis and interpretation of skeletal remains' in P.A. Rahtz, T. Dickinson and L. Watts (eds) 'Anglo-Saxon Cemeteries 1979' *Brit Archaeol Rep* 82 (1980), 221–31. The clavicular degeneration has been attributed by M. Hill (pers comm) to a 'manifestation of the primary occupation of the men of the parish of St Nicholas Shambles: the butchers'. If this were so then the individual cause could have been the carrying of heavy weights on the shoulder, as in handling whole carcasses of sheep and pigs slaughtered on site, *cf.* C. Thawley, 'Butchery Techniques' in Mellor and Pearce, *op. cit.* n25, 175.

62. T. Dyson and J. Schofield, 'Excavations in the City of London: second interim report 1974–1978' *Trans Lon Middx Archaeol Soc* 32 (1981), 78–9; S. Živanovič, *op. cit.* n40, 132; M. Perkins, 'Ancient Diseases' *Popular Archaeol* 4 (1983) 12–15.

63. C. Wells, *op. cit.* n23, 183, n29, 70–1; Dawes, *op. cit.* n6, 58.

64. S. Živanovič, *op. cit.* n40, 88–9.

65. A. Rogers and M. Spector, 'Human stones' *Endeavour* 5 (1981) 119–26.

66. *cf.* C. Wells, *op. cit.* n29, 264 plate 20. The specimen concerned here showed no periostitic reaction to the inflammation of surrounding scalp tissue, *cf.* C. Wells, n23, 164.

67. Harman, Molleson and Price, *op. cit.* n18, 152–3; J. Rogers, I. Watt and P. Dieppe, *op. cit.* n60, 1669. However, at the medieval cemetery of Guildford Friary fractures were absent and at Chelmsford and Stonar healed fractures were very rare: Henderson, *op. cit.* n25, 64.

68. C. Wells, *op. cit.* n29, 131–2.

69. F. Moynihan, 'Disorders of the toes' *The Practitioner* 222 (1979), 30–6; F.A. Symmonds and M.B. Menelaus, 'Hallux valgus in adolescents' *J Bone Joint Surgery* 42B (1960) 761–8; C.H. Barnett, 'The normal orientation of the human hallux and the effect of footwear' *J Anatomy* (1962) 489–94. The condition has been observed at, *inter alia*, the Romano-British cemetery at Poundbury Camp, Dorset, and at the medieval Guildford Friary: T. Molleson, pers. comm.; Henderson, *op. cit.* n25, 67. At these sites the cause of the complaint was thought to be a physiological response to the chronic stress caused by the type of footwear (*viz.* tight leather shoes).

70. H. Ullrich, 'Estimation of fertilty by means of pregnancy and childbirth alterations at the pubis, the ilium and the sacrum' *Ossa* 2 (1975) 23–39; C.A. Holt, 'A re-examination of parturition scars on the female pelvis' *AJPA* 49 (1978) 91–4; M.A. Kelly, 'Parturition and pelvic changes' *ibid.* 51 (1979) 541–5.

71. C. Wells, 'A mediaeval burial of a pregnant woman' *Practitioner* 221 (1978) 442–4.

72. J. Alexander, 'Clopton: the life-cycle of a Cambridgeshire village' in L.M. Mumby (ed) *East Anglian Studies* (1968) 48–70. See also forthcoming publications by A. Boddington and R. Cramp.

73. H.N. Newman and B.G.H. Levers, *op. cit.* n52, 347; C. Wells, *op. cit.* n23 150–1; Tattersall, *op. cit.* n35, 384–5.

74. R.A. Lane and A.J. Sublett, 'Osteology of social organisation: residence pattern' *American Antiquity* 37 (1972) 186–201.

75. Average lifespan for adults as determined from human skeletal remains: Winchester (medieval): male 35.5, female 30.1; Winchester (Saxon): male 36.0, female 29.9; Wharram Percy (medieval): male 35.3, female 31.3 years, respectively, D.R. Brothwell, *op. cit.* n22, 83. For the former there is confirmation from documentary sources of the 13th and 14th centuries, M.M. Postan and J.Z. Titow, 'Heriots and prices on Winchester manors' *Econ Hist Rev* 11 (1985) 392–411; J.R. Longden, 'Note' *ibid* 412–7, quoted in Russell, 'Recent advances in mediaeval demography' n23, 87. More general studies give the 'average length of life' in England as: 31 years (800 AD), 35 (1250), 33 (1450) and 30 (1550 AD): Dublin, Lotka and Spiegelman, quoted in A.E.W. Miles, 'The Dentition of the Anglo-Saxons' *Proc Roy Soc Med* 62 (1969) 881–6. Documentary data are available for the upper classes in English medieval society. Thus, for 97 Londoners born between 1448 and 1520 AD who were members of the livery companies the mean age at death was 49 to 50 years: S.L. Thrupp, *The Merchant Class of Medieval London, 1300–1500* (1948) 194, quoted in T. Dyson and J. Schofield, *op. cit.* n62, 78–9. Similarly, peers summoned to Parliament during the 14th century had a mean age at death 54.7 years and during the 15th century 57.2 years: T.H. Hollingworth, 'A note on the mediaeval longevity of the secular peerage, 1350–1500' *Population Studies* 29 (1975) 156–9; *cf.* J.T. Rosenthal, 'The longevity of the mediaeval English peerage, *ibid.* 27 (1973) 287–93; J.C. Wedgwood, *History of Parliament, 1439–1509, Volume 1: Biographies* (1936) xl.

76. W.J. Moore and E. Corbett, *op. cit.* n49, 141; Bullough and Campbell, *op. cit.* n57, 320–2; P.L. Armitage, A. Davis, V. Straker and B. West, 'Bones, bugs and botany, Part 2' *Popular Archaeol* 4 (1983) 24–7.

77. Newman and Levers, *op. cit.* n52, 347; C. Wells, *op. cit.* n23 150–1.

78. In his contemporary description of the 'most noble city of London' in J. Stow, *Survey of London* (ed C.L. Kingsford, Volume 2 1908), ii, 219–29; D. Brechin, *The Conqueror's London* (1968) 73.

79. F. Barlow, *William Rufus* (1983) 103–4.

80. Unlike contemporary Iceland, where the code of laws in the 11th century (Law of Gulathing) still permitted the infanticide of severely deformed babies: D. Robertson, 'Attitudes towards nutrition and health in the ancient North' *Northern History* 71 (1978) 1562–8.

APPENDIX 1 : CATALOGUE OF SKELETONS

'D' in Burial-Type column indicates disarticulated skeleton

Context No.	DUA No.	Burial Type	Sex	Age	Height (m.)	Cranial Index	Metopism	Wormian Bones	Caries	Abscess	Ante-mortem Loss	Absence
						Normal Variation			Skull		Teeth	
5001	1841	I	F	25–28				X	2/11		3/14	
5002	1842	I	M	21–24	1·78						2/32	
5003	1843	I	M	19–25							2/17	M3
5004	1844	I	F	adult								
5006	1846	I	M	22–25				X				
5008	1847	I	M	35–40				X	2/04			M3
5009	1848	I	F	45+							8/25	
5012	1849	I	M	22–25	1·70							
5013	1850	I	M	adults	1·78							
5014	1851	I	?	12–16								
5014A	1852	I	?	2–3								
5019	2069	D	F	12–18								
5021	1854	I	F	32–35	1·61							M3, P2
5022	2070	I	M	32–35	1·71				1/17		1/18	M3
5023	1855	I	F	25–35				X				
5028	2072	I	M	15–16							2/14	M3
5029	2073	D	?	4–6		X						
5035	2074	I	?	7–8				X			1/16	
5038	1856	I	F	38–45				X				M3
5039	1857	D	F	25–28					2/24			?
5040	1858	I	M	35–38	1·78			X				
5041	1859	I	?	4–5								
5042	1860	II	M	32–35					2/31		2/33	
5047	1862	I	M	17–25	1·78			X				
5049	1863	D	?	adult								
5050	1864	I	F	25–28	1·65				2/22		4/26	M3
5051	1865	I	M	41–45				X	1/21			M3
5052	1866	I	F	17–25								
5053	1867	II	F	41–45	1·56			X	2/29			M3
5057	1870	I	?	infant								
5058	1871	I	F	5–7					4/20			
5059	1872	I	F	25–28	1·63				1/18		4/22	M3

Post-cranial Remains							
Vertebral Osteo-arthritis	Meric Index	Cnemic Index	Other non-metric Variation	Other Dental Anomaly	Cribra	Other Pathology	Context No.
X							5001
X	87·0					periostitis, Rt fibula	5002
X							5003
	93·75						5004
X							5006
							5008
X							5009
X	73·9						5012
							5013
X							5014
							5014A
X			Incisor double-rooted				5019
X							5021
							5022
							5023
							5028
							5029
							5035
							5038
X							5039
X						head of humerus destroyed	5040
							5041
			canine double-rooted		X		5042
						sword wound to cranium	5047
							5049
X	80·7		canine double-rooted		X		5050
	79·6						5051
	81·5						5052
X	73·1						5053
							5057
							5058
X	78·2					skull osteomata	5059

| Context No. | DUA No. | Burial Type | Sex | Age | Height (m.) | Normal Variation | | | Skull | | Teeth | | | |
						Cranial Index	Metopism	Wormian Bones			Caries	Abscess	Ante-mortem Loss	Absence
5061	1873	I	F	23–25	1·56						2/29		?	?,P2
5062	1874	I	?	foetus										
5063	1875	I	M	adult	1·71									
5064	1876	I	F	32–35	1·59									
5065	2076	D	F	adult	1·66									
5066	2077	D	F	6–7										
5067	1877	I	M	adult	1.71									
5068	1878	I	M	17–25	1·71									M3
5070	1879	III	M	45+			X	X			1/23		2/25	M3
5072	2079	II	F	33–35	1·53								3/24	
5073	1880	III	F	25–28	1·25						1/30			
5074	1881	I	F	adult										
5075	1882	I	?	∼9										
5076	1883	I	F	adult									1/27	
5077	1884	I	?	adult										
5078	1885	D	M	∼40				X						
5079	1886	D	M	adult										
5081	1888	I	F	13–16										
5082	1889	I	F	25–28	1·71									
5083	1890	I	F	20–23	1·57									
5084	1891	D	M	adult										
5085	1892	I	M	∼45	1·81			X					2/26	M3
5086	1893	D	F	25–28			X							
5089	1894	I	M	adult	1·75									
5090	1895	I	?	<4½										
5091	1896	I	M	∼25	1·74			I						
5092	1897	I	F	17–18										
5094	1899	II	F	33–35										
5095	1900	I	?	∼1										
5097	1901	D	M	adult										
5098	1902	I	F	11–12			X	X						
5099	1903	I	F	23–25	1·69									
5100	2081	I	F	17–25										
5101	1904	VI	F	25–28	1·64									
5102	1905	D	M	28–32	1·65		X				1/17		1/18	M3

Post-cranial Remains							
Vertebral Osteo-arthritis	Meric Index	Cnemic Index	Other non-metric Variation	Other Dental Anomaly	Cribra	Other Pathology	Context No.
						death in childbirth	5061
							5062
							5063
X			incisor shovelling				5064
X	81·3						5065
							5066
X		78·4			X		5067
	79·4		segmented sternum		X	shoulder o/a	5068
X				molar root hyperplasia			5070
X	71·2		torus palatinus				5072
X		68·6					5073
X			supernumerary tooth			periostitis (left leg)	5074
			incisor shovelling				5075
X							5076
						periostitis, (lower leg)	5077
	81·2						5078
							5079
							5081
	74·9	75·5					5082
							5083
	87·9						5084
X	92·5		Torus palatinus/maxillaris	X		dentistry?	5085
	78·9						5086
							5089
							5090
X	93·8		inca bone	X			5091
							5092
							5094
							5095
							5097
X							5098
							5099
			incisor shovelling				5100
X	79.0			molar root hypercementosis		coxa vara	5101
X	69·5						5102

			Normal Variation			Skull			Teeth			
Context No.	DUA No.	Burial Type	Sex	Age	Height (m.)	Cranial Index	Metopism	Wormian Bones	Caries	Abscess	Ante-mortem Loss	Absence
5103	1906	IV	?	2–3								
5104	1907	I	M	25–31								
5105	1908	I	M	adult	1·70							
5106	2082	I	F	adult								
5107	2083	D	M	adult								
5108	1909	VI	M	20–25	1·66							
5109	1910	I	M	18–22	1·68			X				
5111	1912	I	?	~8								
5112	1913	I	F	39–41	1·59			X				
5115	1914	D	M	40–45	1·66			X				M3
5116	1915	II	M	31–35	1·67							
5117	2084	I	M	adult								
5118	1916	III	M	32–35	1·79			X	3/22		6/30	M3
5119	1917	I	?	juvenile								
5120	1918	I	M	13–15	1·59?							
5121	1919	D	?	adult								
5122	1920	I	F	23–25	1·74							
5123	1921	I	M	17–22	1·65							
5124	1922	I	F	25–28	1·59							
5125	1923	IV	F	38–41			X		2/22	1/22		M3
5126	1924	IV	?	17–19								
5128	1925	I	?	~7				X				
5129	1926	I	?	~2								
5130	1927	I	?	1–1½								
5131	2085	I	M	33–35		71·0		X	1/23		1/24	M3
5133	1928	II	F	33–40					2/23		4/27	M3
5134	1929	IV	F	17–21								
5135	1930	D	?	35–45								
5139	1933	I	?	adult								
5141	1935	I	M	adult	1·64							
5144	1937	III	F	33–35			X	X	2/28		1/29	M3
5147	1938	III	F	22–25		79·4		X			2/19	
5148	1939	II	M	38–41	1·67			X	1/25		2/27	
5149	1940	I	F	adult	1·66?							

Post-cranial Remains							
Vertebral Osteo-arthritis	Meric Index	Cnemic Index	Other non-metric Variation	Other Dental Anomaly	Cribra	Other Pathology	Context No.
							5103
X	77·4					periostitis, Rt fibula	5104
	75·3	77·7					5105
	85·5						5106
							5107
	76·7	77·9					5108
	80·0	76·0					5109
							5111
X							5112
X						Schmorl's nodes	5115
X	86·2	85·7					5116
							5117
X			Torus palatinus/auditivus				5118
							5119
							5120
							5121
						skull osteomata	5122
							5123
	72·3						5124
X							5125
							5126
			bipartite inca bone		X		5128
					X		5129
							5130
			Torus palatinus			parietal osteoporosis	5131
X					X		5133
			incisor shovelling			fractured clavicle	5134
X							5135
							5139
X							5141
X					X	osteoma ('sinus knob')	5144
			incisor shovelling	molar root hyper-cementosis	X	?dentistry	5147
X							5148
X	63·1	72·6					5149

			Normal Variation			Skull			Teeth			
Context No.	DUA No.	Burial Type	Sex	Age	Height (m.)	Cranial Index	Metopism	Wormian Bones	Caries	Abscess	Ante-mortem Loss	Absence
5150	1941	II	F	33–39			X	X		1/22	1/23	
5151	1942	D	M	35–45								
5152	1943	I	?	adolescent								
5153	1944	D	F	adult								
5154	1945	I	F	adult	1·56							
5155	1946	I	F	29–32								
5156	1947	I	F	25–28				X	1/10			
5157	1948	I	F	38–41	1·65	80·2						R
5158	1949	I	F	45+	1·60	74·9		X	1/13		1/14	M3
5159	1950	I	M	adult	1·71							
5162	1952	I	F	<25								
5163	1953	I	M	adult								
5164	1954	I	F	20–24			X	X	1/28		2/30	
5165	1955	II	M	45+	1·66							
5166	1956	I	M	17–25	1·76							
5167	1957	I	?	juvenile								
5168	1958	II	M	25–28	1·69				2/29			M3
5169	2087	I	M	adolescent								
5170	1959	D	?	2–3								
5171	1960	I	?	adult								
5172	1961	II	M	26–45				X	1/14		3/17	M3
5173	1962	I	M	adult								
5174	1963	I	M	adult								
5175	1964	I	M	adult								
5176	1965	IV	M	adult	1·66							
5177	1966	I	M	36–45	1·73							
5178	1967	I	M	adult	1·66							
5179	1968	I	F	∼30								
5180	1969	I	M	adult								
5181	1970	I	F	adult								
5182	1971	I	M	17–25	1·65							
5183	1972	I	M	25–30	1·77							
5185	2088	I	?	adult								
5186	1973	II	F	adult	1·55							
5187	1974	I	M	41–45	1·64				6/15	1/16	4/20	M3

Post-cranial Remains							
Vertebral Osteo-arthritis	Meric Index	Cnemic Index	Other non-metric Variation	Other Dental Anomaly	Cribra	Other Pathology	Context No.
X						periostitis (tibiae)	5150
	85·5	80·0					5151
							5152
							5153
X	85·3						5154
X	82·3	73·3					5155
		71·9				hallux valgus	5156
X	74·9	74·3				o/a of most joints	5157
X	75·4					o/a (joints); C2/C3 fused	5158
	90·0	69·6				periostitis (lower limbs)	5159
							5162
X							5163
	76·5						5164
X						o/a shoulder, knee, ankle	5165
	77·4						5166
							5167
	79·0	73·9					5168
							5169
							5170
							5171
X					X	o/a hip	5172
							5173
							5174
							5175
		76·3					5176
		71·3				healed fracture tibia	5177
X							5178
							5179
		51·2					5180
							5181
	84·0	65·3				periostitis, Rt fibula	5182
X	92·0	80·2					5183
		74·9					5185
	74·2	82·1					5186
X	68·7	65·7					5187

Context No.	DUA No.	Burial Type	Sex	Age	Height (m.)	Cranial Index	Metopism	Wormian Bones	Caries	Abscess	Ante-mortem Loss	Absence
						Normal Variation			Skull		Teeth	
5188	1975	I	F	40–45				X			8/14	
5189	1976	I	F	38–41	1·61	76·8		X		1/30	1/30	
5190	1977	II	F	38–41	1·63	70·4			3/28		2/30	M3
5191	1978	I	M	14–18								M3
5192	1979	I	F	45+	1·61			I			8/30	M3
5193	1980	II	M	12–14				X			2/28	M3
5194	1981	II	F	25–28	1·65			X	3/32			
5195	1982	I	M	35–38		75·5		X			3/24	M3
5196	1983	I	?	6								
5197	2089	I	M	adult	1·74							
5198	1984	I	M	adult	1·69							
5199	2090	I	M	42–45	1·82			X				
5200	1985	I	F	<40	1·57						5/30	P2
5202	1987	I	F	~45	1·57	87·4		X			2/32	
5203	1988	II	F	25–28	1·69							
5204	1989	I	?	8				X				
5205	1990	I	F	~30	1·54							
5206	1991	I	M	45+	1·59							
5207	1992	I	F	45+	1·55	76·6			2/28	1/28	4/32	
5208	1993	I	?	2–4								
5209	1994	I	M	~30	1·65							
5210	1995	II	?	1½								
5211	1996	I	M	~30	1·63							
5212	1997	I	?	1								
5213	1998	I	M	~40	1·71	77·1	X	X				
5215	2000	D	M	45+							12/30	
5216	2001	D	M	45+								
5217A	2002	I	M	17–25	1·62							
5271B	2003	I	M	17–19								
5217C	2004	I	?	juvenile								
5217D	2005	I	?	adult								
5218	2006	I	F	35–45	1·50							
5220	2007	I	M	~30								

| Post-cranial Remains | | | | | | | | |
Vertebral Osteo-arthritis	Meric Index	Cnemic Index	Other non-metric Variation	Other Dental Anomaly	Cribra	Other Pathology	Context No.
X					X		5188
X	73·9	68·2			X		5189
X	76·7	70·0				o/a shoulder, hands, hip	5190
			incisor shovelling				5191
X	62·0	64·5	bipartite inca bone			healed fracture scapula	5192
							5193
	84·7	62·5	L5 free arch				5194
X			canine double-rooted				5195
							5196
	93·7	91·8					5197
X	96·6	64·1				multiple (o/a; fractures arm)	5198
X	70·7					parietal osteoporosis	5199
X	75·2	74·5				periostitis, Rt lower leg	5200
X	78·0		prognathism				5202
	78·9						5203
					X		5204
X	68·3						5205
X	67·2					trauma: lower legs	5206
X	75·6	67·7					5207
							5208
X	70·6					lump on femur neck	5209
							5210
X	86·7	79·0					5211
							5212
X	79·3	63·6	torus palatinus			spina bifida occulta	5213
					X	healed fracture (humerus)	5215
					X		5216
						Schmorl's nodes	5217A
							5217B
	77·6	77·6					5217C
							5217D
	80·4	78·3				parry fracture of radius	5218
X						diaphyseal aclasia	5220

Context No.	DUA No.	Burial Type	Sex	Age	Height (m.)	Cranial Index	Metopism	Wormian Bones	Caries	Abscess	Ante-mortem Loss	Absence
						Normal Variation			Skull		Teeth	
5221	2008	I	?	4								
5222	2009	I	M	17–19	1·69							
5223	2010	I	F	~17								
5224	2011	I	F	30–32	1·61							
5225	2012	I	F	33–35				X	2/20			M3
5226	2091	I	M	adult								
5227	2013	II	?	½								
5228	2014	I	?	infant								
5229	2015	II	M	45+		74·7		X			20/32	
5230	2016	I	M	38+	1·73							
5231	2092	I	?	adult								
5232	2017	I	?	adolescent								
5233	2018	II	F	40–50				X				
5234	2093	I	?	juvenile				X				
5235	2094	I	M	45+					4/21	3/27		M3
5236	2019	D	M	35–45		76·1						
5237	2095	I	M	19–22	1·67	77·7	X	I				
5238	2020	VI	F	38–45	1·62							M3
5239	2021	D	F	25–28	1·57		X	X			1/29	M3
5240	2022	I	F	42–45	1·65			X				M3
5241	2023	I	F	25–28	1·54			X				
5242	2024	D	M	28–32								
5243	2025	VI	M	25–28							4/32	
5244	2027	I	M	28–32	1·67							
5245	2029	I	M	adult								
5246	2030	I	M	35–38				X	2/25			M3
5247	2031	I	?	1–2								
5248	2032	I	M	45+								
5249	2033	I	F	25–28	1·56							
5250	2096	I	?	neonate								
5251	2034	I	M	17–20								
5252	2035	I	?	adult								
5253	2036	I	?	juvenile								
5254	2037	I	?	1½								

Vertebral Osteo-arthritis	Meric Index	Cnemic Index	Other non-metric Variation	Other Dental Anomaly	Cribra	Other Pathology	Context No.
					X		5221
	80·1						5222
	93·8	74·1					5223
	70·5						5224
			L5 free arch				5225
	69·8						5226
							5227
							5228
X							5229
X	80·3						5230
		75·4					5231
		80·2					5232
X							5233
X						parietal osteoporosis	5234
							5235
X			supernumerary tooth			trauma to femoral shaft	5236
	84·3	72·1	inca bone				5237
							5238
	72·4	61·5	supernumerary tooth			Schmorl's nodes	5239
X	85·6		S1 lumbarised			o/a clavicle	5240
	76·5	65·5			X	o/a femoral head	5241
	81·0				X	o/a femoral head & acetabulum	5242
		64·2					5243
X	80·3						5244
							5245
						X	5246
						healed fracture: forearm	5247
							5248
	80·8					healed fracture: forearm	5249
							5250
							5251
							5252
							5253
							5254

			Normal Variation			Skull			Teeth			
Context No.	DUA No.	Burial Type	Sex	Age	Height (m.)	Cranial Index	Metopism	Wormian Bones	Caries	Abscess	Ante-mortem Loss	Absence
5255	2038	I	M	25–28	1·81							
5256	2039	I	F	adult								
5257	2040	III	M	43–45	1·73						1/16	
5258	2041	I	F	35–45								
5259	2042	I	?	1								
5290	2043	IV	?	adult								
5291	2044	I	M	32–35								
5293	2045	I	M	17–22	1·73							
5294	2046	III	M	28–32								
5295	2047	I	?	1½								
5296	2048	I	M	25–28								
5297	2049	D	?	adult								
5299	2050	I	?	juvenile								
5300		I	?	adult								
5301		I	?	adult								
5302		I	?	adult								
5303		I	M	25–28	1·81							
5304		III	M	17–25								
5305		IV	?	juvenile								
5306		IV	M	~40				X	1/29	1/29		
5307		III	F	32–35	1·61							
5308		I	F	25–28	1·66							M3
5309		I	M	17–25								
5310		III	?	juvenile								
5311		II	F	45+	1·62		I		1/14		9/29	M3
5313		I	?	adolescent								
5314		Ia	?	adult								
5316		I	M	28–32	1·67				2/32			
5318		I	?	juvenile								
5319		I	M	adult	1·75							
5322		V	?	infant								

Post-cranial Remains							
Vertebral Osteo-arthritis	Meric Index	Cnemic Index	Other non-metric Variation	Other Dental Anomaly	Cribra	Other Pathology	Context No.
							5255
							5256
							5257
							5258
							5259
						5th metatarsals distorted	5290
							5291
	85·7						5293
						1st metacarpals distorted	5294
							5295
							5296
		66·2					5297
							5299
		69·8				periostitis (both fibulae)	5300
		62·6					5301
	89·7						5302
			S1 lumbarised			Schmorl's nodes	5303
						lump on femur neck	5304
							5305
				second molars unerupted		gallstone	5306
						5th metatarsals distorted	5307
							5308
							5309
							5310
X	69·8		inca bone	molar root hypercementosis			5311
							5313
							5314
X	80·7	69·3	prognathism	molar root hypercementosis		5th metatarsals distorted	5316
							5318
						healed fracture of radius	5319
							5322

APPENDIX 2: PATHOLOGY AND ANOMALIES IN UNSTRATIFIED AND REDEPOSITED BONES

1C	Fused calcaneus/talus (congenital or injury?) (Fig 37)
1	Healed fracture: tibia/fibula fused distally
1097	Healed fracture: humerus mid-shaft
1125	Hip aplasia: congenital absence of left pubis bone, malformed hip-joint (Fig 38)
1134	Healed fracture of humerus
1148	Healed fracture of humerus
3869	Fused calcaneous/talus
3933	Healed fracture of tibia
5018	Metopic skull of a male, greater than 22 years old
5043	Skull of a 7 to 8 year old child with metopism and cribra orbitalia
5093	Skull of an adult female; metopic suture present
5096	Skull of an adult female; missile wound (?) (Fig 52)
5125A	Cranium of a 3-year old child showing cribra orbitalia
5136	Cranium of a 14-year old child showing cribra orbitalia
5140	Metopic skull of a young woman, 17–25 years of age
5143	Juvenile skull showing cribra orbitalia
5161	Skull of adolescent male: metope and shovelled incisors
5201	Cranium of a woman, greater than 40 years old, showing penetrating wound

APPENDIX 3: AN EARLY MEDIEVAL CASE OF DEATH IN CHILDBIRTH

the late Calvin Wells (submitted 1976)

This burial (5061/5062) consists of a female skeleton with the bones of a full term foetus in her abdomen (Figs 57–8). The woman's skeleton, though damaged by post-inhumation erosion, is almost complete down to the middle of her femora. The foetal bones are also virtually complete and in very good condition. The age of this woman at death can be assessed with some confidence as about 22–24 years. This estimate is based upon the appearance of her pubic symphyses, epiphyseal evidence, her dental state, the condition of her cranial sutures, and other details. No gross pathology is detectable anywhere in the skeleton.

The discovery of female burials with unborn infants is not exceedingly rare in ancient cemeteries though it is usually impossible to know whether they can be described as 'obstetric' deaths in the sense of being directly due to some specific hazard of pregnancy, such as eclamptic toxaemia or haemorrhage from a placenta praevia, or whether they were not specifically related to pregnancy but due to such conditions as pneumonia, typhus, plague, tuberculosis, etc. An almost indubitable obstetric death is recorded by Sjøvold *et al.* (1974) from Visby in Gotland where multiple pelvic exostoses were an insuperable barrier to the delivery of a full term foetus

in a young woman aged 17–20 years.

In the St Nicholas Shambles site skeleton which we are discussing here a number of clues point strongly to this also having been an obstetric death. Although no gross pathology is detectable there are a number of features about this burial which are of interest.

The following measurements, in millimetres, were obtainable from the foetus:

	L.	R.
Scapular length	—	?32·3
Humeral length (diaphysis)	66·0	?63·7
Ulnar length (diaphysis)	?52·4	?54·1
Radial length (diaphysis)	—	50·3
Femoral length (diaphysis)	75·9	?74·3
Tibial length (diaphysis)	65·2	—
Fibular length (diaphysis)	?54·7	—

In addition to these there is a rib with a chord length of 56·6 mm.

The above long bone and other measurements are minimal: in most cases evidence of soil erosion of the ends of the diaphyses suggests that they may have been larger by some unknown, albeit small, amount. These figures suffice, however, to show

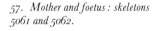

57. Mother and foetus : skeletons 5061 and 5062.

that this was a full term foetus and there seems no doubt that, linearly, it was quite a large one. Despite the absence of any very high correlation between length and weight in newborn infants it is probable that this child weighed not less than 3850 g (8½ lbs) and was quite likely to have been in the 4100–4550 g (9–10 lbs) range.

The distances from the internal auditory meatus to the medial tip of the petrous temporal bone can be measured on both sides and are 13.8 mm (left) and 14.6 mm (right). These are fairly high values and suggest the probability that this was rather a large foetal head with a broad cranial base.

Turning now to the mother, it is unfortunate that the lengths of her femora, tibiae and humeri are not obtainable. Her left ulna and radius have survived in a slightly damaged state but their respective lengths must have been very close to 231 mm and 216 mm. This would be compatible with a stature of about 156 cm (5 ft 2 ins). Evidently she was a smallish woman and this is confirmed by the rest of her surviving bones. The presence of the foetus leaves no doubt about her

sex, nevertheless she had a number of features which, in general, are either strongly masculine or at least somewhat untypical of women. These include a moderately large left mastoid process, moderate brow ridges, a strongly rounded superior orbital border, a rather thick and heavy skull with a much developed external occipital protuberance, a wide frontal sinus extending laterally above both orbits, and a fairly heavily built mandible. All these features are typical of 'android' women, i.e. women whose facial appearance verges towards the masculine pattern. The significance of this is that the condition is presumably due to her hormonal balance and is associated with other android features in other parts of the body—notably the pelvis.

Unfortunately, this women's pelvis is much broken and too deficient to be reconstructible. However, enough survives to show that it had certain android characteristics and was also abnormal in other respects. The posterior part of the iliac crests fall somewhat steeply towards the sacrum—a typically male characteristic (although this feature is masked in Figs 57–8).

The greater sciatic notches, although within the female range of angle, are sufficiently narrow to overlap what is often found in male pelves. The superior surface of the first sacral vertebral segment is about 47.1 mm in transverse diameter which together with the surviving fragments of the alae, might suggest that the whole width of the sacrum was rather narrow. More significantly, perhaps, the iliac bones are narrow and markedly asymmetrical. The antero-posterior diameter of the left innominate from the antero-inferior iliac spine to the posterior iliac spine is 133.7 mm, i.e. the so-called 'false' (or upper) pelvic cavity seems to have been small and this is likely to have been associated with what obstetricians call a short 'true conjugate', which is the length of the antero-posterior entrance to the lower part of the pelvic cavity.

The sacro-iliac joints, as shown by their well preserved surfaces on the innominate bones, were extremely asymmetrical. The right articular surface measures 58.3 mm vertically by 17.4 mm in maximum breadth, thus giving a breadth-height index of 29.8%. The left side measures 45.2 × 27.8 mm, giving an index of 61.5%. Moreover, the right sacro-iliac joint is set very far forward on the ilium. Its anterior border is only 14.5 mm from the apex of the greater sciatic notch. This is further evidence of the markedly forward position of the sacrum and the probability of restricted entry to the pelvic cavity. Further asymmetry of the innominate bone is shown by a markedly irregular area of craggy bone which projects medially from the right ilium just behind its auricular (i.e. articular) surface.

The sum of this evidence suggests, therefore, that we have here a small woman with a number of android features in her skull and pelvis combined with certain pelvic deformities, who had reached the end of her pregnancy carrying a large foetus which possibly had an unusually broad head. Until well into the present century this was a situation which often constituted an obstetrician's 'nightmare'.

We cannot positively know that this woman died in childbirth but with a foetus of this size it is extremely likely that her labour had started. A study of Fig 57 provides further clues. Not only does it confirm the narrowness of the sacrum and reveal the asymmetry of the ilia but it also shows that the large foetal head lies across the brim of the 'true' pelvic cavity, apparently slightly wedged into it. To anyone with obstetric experience this must suggest that the woman had been in labour for several hours, perhaps days, and that the disproportion between foetal head and pelvis had eventually led to the onset of secondary uterine inertia when her exhausted uterine muscle could no longer continue the struggle to push this large baby through an inadequate pelvic canal. Death from maternal exhaustion would have been the result. It is perhaps worth noting that neither the area around her pubic symphysis nor her preauricular grooves show any evidence of previous pregnancy and we may reasonably infer, therefore, that she was a primipara.

References

Hawkes SC and Wells C, 1975 'An Anglo-Saxon obstetric calamity from Kingsworthy, Hampshire' *Medical and Biological Illustration* **25** 47–51.

Sjøvold T, Swedborg I, and Diener L, 1974 'A pregnant woman from the middle ages with exostosis multiplex' *Ossa* **1** 3–23.

Trotter M, and Gleser GC, 1952 'Estimation of stature from long bones of American whites and negroes' *AJPA* **10** 436–514.

APPENDIX 4: A TOOL FOR COPING WITH JUVENILE HUMAN BONES FROM ARCHAEOLOGICAL EXCAVATIONS

Rosemary Powers (submitted 1979)

Most methods of ageing juvenile bones have been developed on living populations, and are inapplicable to archaeological bones because these are often incomplete, mixed or out of context. I have therefore sought a method which can cope with these problems.

Archaeological skeletal examinations need comparative series. No chart exists of measurements of immature skeletons of known age. Ideally such a chart should be based on averaged measurements from representative series of individuals as are the growth curves of the living (eg Tanner 1977), but the available skeletons of known age are far too few to allow this. It was therefore necessary to use individual skeletons.

It is impractical to extrapolate from the living to skeletal series; even if radiographs are used with due allowance for measurement errors caused by parallax, comparison with skeletons is difficult. The amount of shrinkage of bone after burial is unknown, though it is presumed to be negligible on the basis of studies on the denser adult bones. 'Landmarks' present on the skeleton are not available on the living body and vice-versa. Another drawback is that modern standards of health and nutrition allow practically all individuals to reach their maximum growth potential, whereas the earlier populations excavated by archaeologists undoubtedly include many with retarded growth. Such individuals might also be over-represented in cemetery samples since they would be more likely to die at an earlier age.

Therefore I have used the measurements of the few European children of known age at death to which I have had access over the years (Fig 59), to build up a chart based solely on the measurements obtainable from the separated bones of the skeleton (Fig 60). Although based on limited samples, it has proved an invaluable tool for dealing with imperfect and mixed archaeological material and I have been asked to publish it by other workers in this field.

The bones are listed across the top of the chart in approximately descending order of their growth potential. The length of each individual measurement is plotted downwards from this on mm-squared graph paper, *actual size* (NB Fig 60 is a reduction of actual size). The measurements of each individual are connected by lines (dotted across gaps) and the age (real and dental) filled in, where known, in column 1 against the femur length. The chart can be used like a ruler, laying the identified long-bone on the appropriate column, one end on the top line, and reading off the nearest ages to its lower end. The measurements of the bones of each skeleton are joined by a zig-zag line with a general tendency to slope upwards, because the bones are arranged in diminishing size sequence and the well-known cline in rate of growth between head and feet makes this slope change with developmental age regardless of the overall size of the individual.

There is a great shortage of immature skeletons of known age, but I have had the use of the following three sources in London:

(1) The Royal College of Surgeons of England collection of dried foetal skeletons (Hunterian and later acquisitions), the most complete specimen being used for each age group. The origins of the specimens are not recorded but Hunter's material was prepared between 1750 and 1790, Macmurdo's was obtained in Paris before 1857, and the rest collected between these dates, probably from Britain. The ages were estimated on development by comparison with fresh material of known history by the curators who compiled the catalogue. The skeletons are defleshed but dried with cartilage holding the bones together. As the tips of the bones were masked by this dried cartilage there is probably up to 1 mm measuring error. These specimens are still at the Royal College of Surgeons, and Miss Jessie Dobson, former curator of the Hunterian Museum, arranged for me to measure them shortly before her retirement.

(2) St Bride's Fleet Street columbarium provided

Age	Sex	RCS No.	Fe	Tb	Fl	Hm	Ul	Ra	Mdb	Ib	Ih	Clv	Ex	M	FcB	Rb
Foetus 6 weeks		1	2	2	—	2	2	2	5	—	—	4	—	—	0·5	—
Foetus 7 weeks		1·1	5	6·5	—	6·5	6·5	6·5	10	1	1	7	—	—	—	—
Foetus 4 months		6	14	13	13	14·5	13	13	14·5	7	7	13	—	—	1·5	1
Foetus 4 months		7	20	16	15	19	17	17	19	9	9	17·5	—	—	2	1
Foetus 5 months		10	27	24	24	27	23·5	23·5	23	12	12	21	—	—	2	1
Foetus 6 months		17	36	33	30·5	33	33	28	27	17	25	25	—	—	2·5	2·5
Foetus 6 months		19	45	39	36·5	40	37	33	33	17	16	16	—	11·5	4	2
Foetus 6–7 months		22	52	46	44	46	44	40	34	20	20	30·5	—	12	5	5
Foetus 7 months		25	57·5	50	49	50	48	43	38	28	25	39	—	—	5	2
Foetus 8 months		28	70	64	64	62	59	53	47	32	30	41	—	—	6	3
Birth		30	74	64	62	67	60	53	51	37	35	44	—	—	6	6
Birth		32	71	59	58	62	59	52	50	30	29·9	41	—	—	5	4
Birth		42·2	79	62	60	64	56	51	—	34	34	46	—	25	6	4·5
1 year 2 months	M	73	118	100	—	94	76	71	72·5	53	49	55	—	—	10	7
1 year 10 months	F	125	150	123	—	116	97	86	—	68	58	69	—	—	14	8
2 years	F	125	190	152	150	138	112	101	78	76	68	74	—	—	13	7
3 years 7 months	F	181	188	148	—	146	113	103	84	80	68	75	—	—	14·5	8
7 years 3 months	M rickets	73	216	170	—	169	126	—	96	95	78	89	—	—	19	9
6 years 11 months	M	75	232	191	192	170	135	125	93·5	99	85	85	—	39 spina bifida	17	9
6 years	M	44	244	190	189	176	145	—	100	85	95·	90	—	39 fused neck and pelvis	—	9
8 years	M	89	267	221	219	196	—	149	94	98	83	80	—	—	18	10
8 years 11 months	F	Anne Mowbray	279	220	210	185	148	140	—	89	82	82	—	—	17	9
14 years	F	53	349	289	280	265	212	190	106	121	115	128	—	48	21·5	12
14 years	M	113	364	297	296	244	208	179	117	123	111	—	—	41·5	22	15
20 years	M	154	385	315	—	—	232	201	—	139	118 fused	—	—	—	27	13
17 years	M	96	395	315	302	270	235	206	121	142	107	128	—	48	24	16

59. *Measurements of bones of selected medieval European children at death (in mm). For key, see Fig 60.*

a series of individuals in which the bones were separated and the age and other details were available from the associated coffin plates. The age is usually given to the nearest year but a few give the exact age. Unfortunately, most of the two-year-olds have been mixed in one box since discovery, so their exact identity is unknown, although the larger bones have been sorted into skeletons by the use of this chart, plus differences in preservation and pathology. I was allowed to measure these by special permission of the Rector,

Reverend Dewi Morgan. The dates of interment range from 1766 to 1840, virtually the same time-range as the Royal College of Surgeons series.

(3) Anne Mowbray's skeleton, though from an earlier period (d. 1481) has been included. Her exact age at death is known (8 yr 11 months), which is so unusual for a child of the period that it is unlikely that any more medieval child skeletons of known age will be found with which to compare her. Due to the generosity of Dr Francis

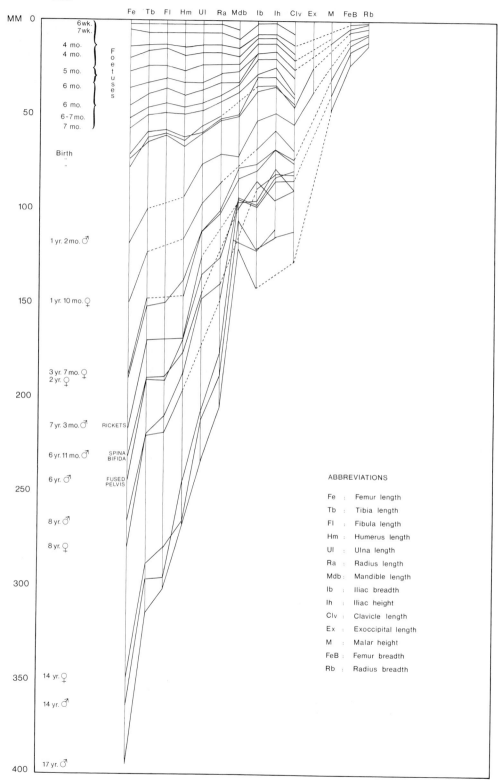

Celoria, I was allowed to measure her bones the day before they were re-interred. I unfortunately did not take the mandibular measurement as the mental symphysis was fused, and the exoccipital measurement could not be taken as the exoccipital suture was likewise obliterated. Her dental age was unusually retarded in some respects and this is correlated with congenital absence of the left second molars and presumably the third molars also.

Ageing on dental development is reasonably accurate and is applicable to even fragmentary remains. However, post-cranial bones cannot always be certainly associated with jaws. To determine maximum length of the bones measured, an engineer's sliding caliper accurate to 0.5 mm was used throughout. Greater accuracy was pointless, since post-mortem decay produced errors of this order. Diaphyses of long-bones can usually be identified even at the foetal stage (however, care is required since the femur and humerus can be confused in very young foetuses). The ilium can usually be identified, which is particularly useful since it can establish whether incomplete bones are in fact human. Both the maximum diameters of the ilium were taken in the unrealised hope that consistent sex differences would show up. As the clavicle and mandible are the earliest bones to ossify (at about two months *in utero*), they also justified inclusion. The exoccipital, a characteristic bean-shaped unit bearing the occipital condyle was found to survive intact better than any other cranial element in foetal and infant bones, so was included although it fuses at about 6 years, and is therefore useless in the older age groups. The mandible, useful because it links teeth and skull development, also fuses at the symphysis at about 6 years but is still measureable if the measurement is taken from the condyle to the tip of the chin in older children, and is simply measured as a long-bone in the younger ones where the rami are still separate. Measurements on archaeological series can, of course, be plotted against dental age, but to some extent this risks a circular argument as malnutrition is known to delay both dental and skeletal maturation.

The maximum breadth of each long-bone at the mid-point was also taken. This was only a rough guide to age but was useful for very frag-

mentary material. Only the forearms and main leg bones are included in the graph.

I have hesitated to combine specimens from very diverse populations (e.g. from Britain and Ceylon) because known differences in adult body proportions presuppose differences in the growth rates of the various elements of the skeleton. Thus the charts show severe gaps, some of which cannot be filled and which reflect the remarkable survival of pre-adolescent children once they are past infancy. Incomplete as they are, however, the charts have proved useful in several ways.

Age estimation on size

Direct ageing is probably better reflected in the degree of slope of the plotted graph than in the skeleton's overall size, particularly when different populations are involved. The differences in size between the sexes at each age-group can be either useful or confusing according to circumstances. There is a period when girls are ahead of boys, though they start and finish growth as the smaller sex.

Mixed skeletons

If several skeletons are mixed it is usually possible to sort them out by plotting the parts of the graph matrix, where the course of the joining lines should become evident. This is particularly valuable in connecting the mandible (and hence the dentition) with the rest of the skeleton. Likewise, archaeological 'scatter' can be assigned to its probable origin, and intrusive bones detected.

Recognition of growth disorders

Children showing disorders affecting growth show up surprisingly strongly by deformities in the shape of the graph line, relative to others. This was not only true of dwarfing conditions like rickets but also in what looked at first sight like localised defects, such as ischio-pubic fusion and sacro-lumbar spina bifida.

Many similar charts have been constructed in the course of study of archaeological series, such as those from Cannington and Winchester, but are not reproduced here. The writer hopes that other workers in the field will find the idea helpful and that those with access to suitable material will incorporate their data into the graph for general use.

Findings using the method

Professor Richard Wright, of Sydney University,

60. Chart of measurements to age children's bones (50% reduction from the original size).

used my chart on an archaeological series. He obtained a copy of 'Human Growth and Development' by R. McCammon (1970) which gives average long-bone lengths for modern children plotted against known age. Professor Wright's comparison of femur length (the only measurement directly comparable with mine) in the 9 cases of comparable age shows in 8 cases out of the 9 approximately two year's retardation in my 'historical' cases by modern standards. The dental retardaton appears to be about 6 months, within the margin of error advised by the Schour and Massler charts, but appears consistent. Greater retardation probably results in obvious bands of enamel hypoplasia, such as occur in cases of rickets (St. Bride's).

I have amassed dozens of measurements of archaeological immature skeletons which give a similar picture of small bones relative to the state of dental development. Recent work in under-developed countries has produced the oft-quoted generalisation that chronically under-nourished children may be as much as two years behind their fully-nourished contemporaries in skeletal growth. The dental eruption is also delayed, but to a lesser extent (see e.g. Trowell, 1960).

AUTHOR'S ACKNOWLEDGEMENT

Particular thanks are due to Shirley Jarman and Mary Harman for their advice and encouragement, and to the Reverend Dewi Morgan, Miss Jessie Dobson and Dr Francis Celoria for the privilege of access to the skeletons in their care. I am also grateful to Robert Kruszynski (British Museum, Natural History) for his great patience and care in checking all the measurements and drawing the chart for publication, and to Nick Griffiths (Museum of London) for his subsequent work on the illustration.

References

Tanner JM, 1977 *Human Biology, An introduction to Human Evolution, Variation, Growth and Ecology* Part **IV** 299–360.

McCammon R, 1970 *Human Growth and Development*.

Trowell HC, 1960 *Non-infective Disease in Africa*.

Schour I and Masler M, 1941 The Development of the Human Dentition, *J. Amer Dent Assc* **28**, 1153–1160.

Scheuer JL, Musgrave JH and Evans SP, 1980 The estimation of the late foetal and perinatal age from limb bone length by linear and logarithmic regression, *Annals of Human Biology* **7**, No.3: 257–265.

SUMMARIES IN FRENCH AND GERMAN

Resumé

Une fouille du Musée de Londres de l' époque médiévale a exposé en 1975–77 deux cent trente-quatre squelettes. Ils proviennent du cimetière de la paroisse de St Nicholas Shambles, près de New-gate Street dans la Cité de Londres. Ils datent du 11ème et 12ème siècles. On a distingué dans le cimetière six types de tombes dont la majorité était des sépultures simples, la présence de cercueils n'a pu être définitivement établie bien que des fragments de bois aient été trouvés dans plusieurs tombes.

Les données démographiques et ostéologiques ont été comparées avec celles d'autres groupes de la même époque. On a trouvé que les mesures extrêmes et moyennes de la taille des individus étaient comparables avec ces populations. Les crânes sont d'une forme intermédiaire entre le crâne dolicéphale des anglo-saxons (à tête allongée) et les crânes du Moyen-Age plus récents de type brachycéphale (à tête ronde). Certaines caractéristiques cranières et dentaires indiquent qu'il y avait peut-être des sous-groupes familiaux dans cette population.

On a trouvé peu de preuves de maladie des os. La reconstitution des dentitions a permis de faire un bilan sur la santé globale de ce groupe. Les maladies dues à la malnutrition telle l'ostéoporose étaient présentes, ainsi que les déformations osseuses peut-être dues à l'anémie causée par une alimentation déficiente en fer. Plusieurs squelettes avaient des traces d'ostéoarthrite causant une dégénérance des os portant sur la plupart des articulations et surtout sur la colonne vertébrale. Un type de malformation de la colonne vertébrale était quatre fois plus fréquent parmi les hommes que parmi les femmes et était peut-être causé par le port de lourds fardeaux. Il y avait peu de tumeurs cancéreuses sur les squelettes, peu de preuves de maladies infectieuses telle la tuberculose et aucune trace de la maladie de Paget. En général, on a noté la présence de peu de blessures ou de fractures survenues durant la vie des individus. Les cas individuels dignes d'être notés comprenaient un homme d'âge moyen avec un bras droit en mauvais état dont l'articulation de l'épaule avait été abîmée lors d'une maladie probablement contractée pendant son enfance. Un autre homme plus jeune avait souffert d'un désordre de croissance qui avait empêché le développement normal de ses membres. Une jeune fille dont la jambe gauche manquait, avait vécu assez longtemps pour atteindre l'adolescence et une autre, de grande taille et probablement trop grosse, devait boiter fortement. Le demi squelette d'une femme morte en couches est à noter spécialement. Plusieurs squelettes avaient des caractéristiques communes ce qui laisse penser qu'ils appartenaient à des individus de la même famille. L'analyse du cimetière démontre qu'il existe des groupes familiaux.

Bien que cet article précède la publication détaillée de la description de l'église et de la disposition topographique du cimetière, il fait l'étude provisoire des divers types de tombes et des preuves de l'existence de rituels d'enterrement.

Zusammenfassung

Im früh-mittelalterlichen Friedhof der Kirche St Nicholas Shambles an der Newgate Street in der City of London wurden 234 Skelette gefunden, deren Gebeine noch bei einander lagen. Sie wurden 1975–77 vom Museum of London ausgegraben. Nach archäologischen Daten stammen sie aus dem 11. und 12. Jahrhundert. Sechs Arten von Gräbern wurden unterschieden. Obwohl viele einzelne Holzteile gefunden wurden, konnten Särge nicht mit Sicherheit nachgewiesen werden.

Demographische und osteologische Daten wurden verglichen mit solchen mittelalterlicher Bevölkerung von anderswo, wobei die Reihen der Grössen der Menschen übereinstimmte. Die Schädelform lag zwischen anglo-sächsischen *doli-*

cephaly, 'Langschädeln' und späteren, mittelalterlichen *bracycephaly*, 'Rundköpfen'. Einige Eigenarten der Schädel und Zähne wiesen auf verwandtschaftliche Gruppen in der Gemeinde hin.

Die Knochen enthielten nicht viele Anzeichen von Krankheiten. Der Aufbau der Zähne gewährte einen Einblick in den allgemeinen Gesundheitszustand der Bevölkerung. Es zeigten sich Schäden in Form von Anämie, wahrscheinlich in Folge von Eisenmangel. Die meisten Knochen hatten Anzeichen von Artritis, Degeneration-serscheinungen an den meisten Gelenken, besonders jedoch an der Wirbelsäule. Eine Form dieses Knochenbefalls zeigte sich viermal öfter bei Männern als bei Frauen, was auf das Tragen schwerer Lasten zurückgeführt wurde. Krebstumor war selten und nicht bösurtig. Keine Anzeichen für Tuberkulose wurden registriert. Pagetsche Krankheit existierte nicht. Im Allgemeinen zeigten sich nur wenige Verwundungen, auch Brüche waren selten. Im Einzelfall hatte ein Mann im mittleren Alter einen schwer beeinträchtigten rechten Arm, (die deformierte Schulter erhielt er wahrscheinlich durch eine Krankheit in seiner Kindheit.) Bei einem jüngeren Manne zeigten sich Entwicklungsstörungen, die das Wachstum seiner Glieder beeinträchtigt hatten. Ein Mädchen mit einem Bein war gestorben bevor sie 20 Jahre alt war und ein anderes, großes und wahrscheinlich übergewichtiges hatte stark gehinkt. Besonders beachtenswert war der Teil eines Skeletts einer Frau, die im Kindbett gestorben war.

Die hohe Anzahl spezifischer Charakterzüge der Knochen läßt auf die Verwandtschaft vieler der Verstorbenen schließen. Die Analyse des Friedhofs brachte Hinweise auf mögliche Familiengruppierungen.

Im Voraus zur ausführlichen Veröffentlichung der Ausgrabungsresultate der Kirche und ihrer Lage zum Friedhof wird hier eine vorläufige Einführung der verschiedenen Gräbertypen gegeben, zusammen mit möglichen Anzeichen für Beerdigungszeremonien.